MEDIUM AEVUM MONOGRAPHS

MEDIUM AEVUM MONOGRAPHS XLII

THOMAS AGNI DA LENTINI

VITA SANCTI PETRI MARTIRIS

CURAVIT

DONALD PRUDLO

The Society for the Study of Medieval Languages and Literature

OXFORD 2022

THE SOCIETY FOR THE STUDY OF MEDIEVAL

LANGUAGES AND LITERATURE

OXFORD, 2022

http://aevum.space/monographs

ISBN-13:

978-1-911694-09-0 (pb)
978-1-911694-10-6 (hb)
978-1-911694-11-3 (pdf)

British Library Cataloguing in Publication Data

A catalogue record for this book is available from the British Library

To Russel Lemmons, Distinguished Scholar,
Defender of the Humanities, and Friend

CONTENTS

INTRODUCTION

The *Vita Sancti Petri Martiris* was the official life of St. Peter of Verona, commissioned by the Order of Preachers (the Dominicans), and entrusted to the authorship of Thomas Agni of Lentini.[1] St. Peter of Verona had been a famous and charismatic preacher of the Dominican order. Entering during the first generation of friars, he proved to be an able administrator and trusted official for both the Dominicans and the papacy. Because of this, he enjoyed increasing levels of responsibility, until he was finally appointed papal inquisitor for the territory of Lombardy in central Italy in late 1251. Less than a year later, he was murdered by a conspiracy of Cathars and their sympathizers.[2] Not a year after that, he received the honor of canonization under Pope Innocent IV (r. 1243–1254), becoming not only the second saint of the young order but its effective protomartyr.[3] Peter's cult became widely and quickly diffused throughout the Christian world due to a combination of papal predilection, the Christendom-wide presence of the Order of Preachers, and genuine popularity. Early efforts to memorialize him

---

[1] The legislation of the General Chapter of Pisa, 1276: "We will and command that the legend of blessed Peter Martyr, composed by the venerable Patriarch of Jerusalem at the request of the Master of the order, be kept in every convent and, so that this might be observed, we wish the provincial priors to be diligent regarding this ordinance." *Acta capitulorum generalium Ordinis Praedicatorum*, eds. Benedikt Maria Reichert and Franz Andreas Frühwirth, 9 vols (Rome: In domo generalitia, 1898), vol. 1, 188.

[2] For a comprehensive analysis of Peter's life and cult see my book, *The Martyred Inquisitor: The Life and Cult of Peter of Verona* (Aldershot: Ashgate, 2008); with some further considerations in "The Assassin-Saint: The Life and Cult of Carino of Balsamo", *The Catholic Historical Review* 94, no. 1 (2008): 1–21.

[3] The Martyrs of Avignonet, who were killed in 1242, never generated much of a cult, nor could they successfully navigate the road to canonization, most likely because they lost their lives during a long papal interregnum.

included the Bull of canonization *Magnis et crebris*,[4] the Dominican
liturgy of Humbert of Romans standardized in 1256,[5] many sermons
preached on his feast day, and the Dominican work of historical
self-reflection by Gerard de Frachet called the *Vitas fratrum* (compiled
between 1256 and 1259).[6] None of these texts, however, was a
comprehensive medieval *legendum*. Between 1263 and 1266, Jacopo
da Varazze completed the first version of his *Golden Legend* and
included a section on the life and miracles of his Dominican
confrère.[7] Around the same time, the Master of the Order, most likely
John of Vercelli (r. 1263–1283), commissioned Thomas Agni of
Lentini to write the official version of Peter's story for dissemination
and preservation among the Dominicans. This effort of the orders to
"control the message" about their saints was not unusual. The
Franciscans had declared Minister General Bonaventure's life of St.
Francis definitive in 1263 and ordered all previous versions of the life
of their founder destroyed in 1266.[8] On the Preachers' part, Humbert
of Romans had written a new life of the founder at some point

4   Innocent IV, "Magnis et Crebris," [24 March 1253], *Bullarium ordinis fratrum
     Praedicatorum*, ed. Thomas Ripoll, 7 vols (Rome: Ex typographia Hieronimi
     Mainardi, 1729), vol. 1, 228-230; translated in *The Martyred Inquisitor*, 191-195.
     Most recently edited and translated into French in: Patrick Gilli, *Le
     gouvernement pontifical et l'Italie des villes au temps de la théocratie: (fin XIIe -
     mi-XIVe s.)* (Montpellier: Presses Univ. de la Méditerranée, 2010), 637-652.

5   William R. Bonniwell, *A History of the Dominican Liturgy* (New York: J.F.
     Wagner, Inc, 1944).

6   Gérard de Frachet, O.P., *Vitae fratrum Ordinis Praedicatorum*, ed. Benedict
     Maria Reichert, O.P., MOPH 1 (Louvain: E. Charpentier & J. Schoonjans,
     1896).

7   Iacopus de Voragine, *Legenda aurea*, ed. Giovanni Paolo Maggioni, 2 vols
     (Florence, 1998), 475-493.

8   John Moorman, *A History of the Franciscan Order from Its Origins to the Year
     1517* (Oxford: Clarendon Press, 1968), 152 n1.

between 1246 and 1248.[9] When he became Master he issued a command that this new *vita* was to be inserted in all the lectionaries, and that new attempts to write lives of Dominic were forbidden.[10] Such efforts were not only to centralize the presentation of the orders' saints, but to standardize materials for preaching, and to maintain some supervision over the contents so that dubious stories and miracles could be excised.

Master John of Vercelli likewise wanted an official recounting of the life of Peter of Verona, and commissioned Thomas Agni of Lentini to accomplish the task. He was chosen for several reasons. In the first place he was an Italian of the Roman province, and may have had personal contact with the saint (though this is not historically certain). He was a well known preacher and writer, and many of his sermons have survived, two of which became attached as prefaces to the *Vita Sancti Petri Martiris* in various manuscripts. Most probably, the order selected him because he was one of its most prominent members, having served in various official capacities both within the order and in the wider Church.[11] He was a native of Lentini in Sicily, on the outskirts of Catania. Having joined the order at an early date, Pope Gregory IX (r. 1227–1241) sent him as a preacher to Naples where, in 1231, he established the Dominican presence in the city at the convent of Sant'Arcangelo, which was to become the famous San Domenico Maggiore in later years. While there he had to endure the enmity of Emperor Frederick II towards the Church in general and the mendicant orders in particular. As King of Sicily, Frederick

---

[9]   With later emendations that became the order's official vita for the founder in 1256, see, Simon Tugwell, *Humberti de Romanis: Legendae Sancti Dominici* (Rome: Institutum Historicum Fratrum Praedicatorum, 2008), 53-56.

[10]   *Acta*, 1. 105.

[11]   In spite of his contemporary prominence, the details of his life and activities are sparse, see the entry "Tommaso Agni" in the *Dizionario biografico degli italiani* (Treccani, 1960); and Stefano Orlandi, *San Pietro Martire da Verona: Leggenda di fra' Tommaso Agni da Lentini nel volgare trecentesco* (Florence: Sansoni, 1952), XVLII-LIV. See also Stephen de Salagnac and Bernard Gui, *De quattuor in quibus Deus praedicatorum ordinem insignavit*, ed. Thomas Käppeli, MOPH 22 (Rome, 1949), 91 n8; 114 n2.

expelled members of the convent who were not natives of the *Regno* (his lands which included Sicily and the southern third of the Italian peninsula). This left Thomas as prior of a convent which included only himself and the elderly John of San Giuliano. To this small band a not insubstantial addition was soon made when, in the early 1240s, Thomas Aquinas made his Dominican profession into Thomas Agni's hands.[12] Recognizing Thomas Agni's talents, the order appointed him an elector of Master Humbert at the Budapest chapter of 1254. He served as *lector* and *diffinitor* several times and finally received appointment as the Prior provincial of the Roman province from 1255 until 1256. Alexander IV (r. 1254–1261) nominated him Bishop of Bethlehem in the Holy Land sometime after 1256, but certainly by 1259. This mission thrust him into the confused politics of the remaining Crusader interests, the Italian city-states, and the military orders. He worked tirelessly to promote peace among the warring factions. He excommunicated Bohemond VI of Antioch for his alliance and submission to the Mongols. In all this, Agni apparently acquitted himself with credit, for he was recalled from the Holy Land by Urban IV (r. 1261–1264) who named him papal vicar of the city of Rome on 13 Feb 1264. Agni proved himself very able at ingratiating himself with every successor of Peter he encountered, and Pope Clement IV (r. 1265–1268) raised him to the dignity of Archbishop of Cosenza in Calabria on 18 Apr 1267. Thomas had not yet reached the height of his honors however. The next pope, Gregory X (r. 1271–1276), appointed Thomas as the Latin Patriarch of Jerusalem on 19 Mar 1272. A month later he made him papal legate to the Holy Land and commissioned him to co-ordinate the naval reinforcement of the Levant. One could imagine this office was much more of a burden than an honor for the Dominican friar. The Kingdom of Jerusalem was tottering on the brink of disaster, having lost most of its territory outside the city of Acre, and the endemic rivalries between the Italian maritime cities and the military orders had still not ceased. Menaced by the Mamluks and Mongols alike,

---

[12] Donald Prudlo, *Thomas Aquinas: A Historical, Theological, and Environmental Portrait* (Mahwah, NJ: Paulist, 2020), 66-67.

there was little help that came from the west, despite his tireless efforts. Not even the aid of Prince Edward of England and the Ninth Crusade (1271–1272) brought much respite. It is likely that Agni's repeated petitions to the leaders of the west made the relief of the Holy Land one of the three main priorities of the Second Council of Lyons in 1274. Unable to reconcile all the warring factions, Agni died at some point during the last half of the month of September 1277. Certainly the luster of such an eminent Dominican personage – probably the highest ranking Dominican between Cardinal Hugh of St. Cher (d. 1253) and Pierre Tarentaise (Pope Innocent V, r. 1276) – lent significant prestige to the *Vita* of St. Peter.[13]

During the period of this work's composition the Dominican order was going from one success to the next. Following the canonization of Peter in 1253, they triumphantly concluded their campaign against the secular clergy at the University of Paris in 1256. Enjoying increasing papal prestige they found themselves appointed in growing numbers to trusted positions in the Church, as the career of Thomas Agni shows plainly. This was also the period of the dawning success of Dominican scholasticism, spearheaded by Albert the Great and Thomas Aquinas. These were only the two most famous names among a profusion of brilliant scholars exercising their talents in nearly every field of academic endeavor. During this period the Preachers were also extending their supervision over the various inquisitions then present in various regions of Europe, while at the same time cultivating good relations with monarchs throughout Christendom. New Dominican foundations were springing up from the Baltic countries to Spain, from Scandinavia to Cyprus and the Holy Land, not to mention missions that spread into the near east among the Cumans, Mongols, and Armenians. The astonishing ascendance that the order had achieved in the half century of its existence would be confirmed when, in 1276, one of its own number was elected as Pope Innocent V (though he ruled for less than half a year). The Church at large had also achieved a position of significant

---

[13] One could argue a similar eminence for Cardinal Annibale d'Annibaldi, who was Cardinal-Priest of Dodici Apostoli between 1262 and 1272, but he was a Master of Theology, and it seems he was never raised to the rank of Bishop.

supremacy over European society. Bolstered by a string of clever, strong, and innovative pontiffs, the Roman Church had emerged victorious in its struggle with the German empire, and its moral authority was at a high point. With its mendicant allies spread throughout Christendom, the papacy was able to exercise authority in a manner unavailable to previous generations. All of this served as the external context for the composition of the *Vita*.

In the period between the death of Peter and the composition of this *Vita*, the saint's fame had already spread throughout Christendom, with miracles being reported as far away as Ireland and the Atlantic coast of Spain. While his cult was certainly aided by the well-travelled Dominicans and bolstered by repeated reminders of papal solicitude, it was also genuinely popular. From the day of his death, medieval people flocked to his bier and eventual tomb at Sant' Eustorgio in Milan, making it a center of pilgrimage and miracle-seeking. As a martyr, one of a select class in the middle ages, Peter's appeal was spontaneous and enduring. One need only look at the fame of the cult of Thomas Becket at Canterbury.[14] Contemporary martyrs were rare and highly valued by the Christian community. Such a combination was irresistible. In that sense Peter's story was already diffused by the Bull of Canonization, as well as Dominican liturgy and preaching, not to mention the many new churches and altars dedicated to him throughout the Christian world.[15] Therefore Thomas Agni's *vita* was not meant to be a piece necessarily designed for the spread and cultivation of Peter's devotion in the outside world, but rather to be seen as part of the order's efforts to streamline his

---

[14] For a comparative analysis of the cults of the two saints see my "Martyrs on the Move: The Spread of the Cults of Thomas of Canterbury and Peter of Verona," *Peregrinations* 3.2, Summer 2011.

[15] Dozens of altars in Dominican churches and many foundations under his patronage reflect the spread of his devotion. This in turn led to the founding of many lay confraternities, *laude* and prayers in his honor, artistic commissions, civic legislation of his devotion in many cities, popular expressions of faith in his contact relics, miracle stories, and namings in his honor. This elision of Dominican and lay piety is traced in detail in chapters 4 and 5 of my *Martyred Inquisitor*.

cultic presentation, and to have a common text for preaching, reading, and devotional study within the convents of the Preachers. Likely intended for internal consumption then, this *Vita* is significant because it gives us a snapshot of Dominican self-reflection in the 1260s and 70s.[16] Peter had been a popular and charismatic figure, visibly and almost aggressively public throughout his entire career. Dominic on the other hand had been the bearer of a quieter sort of holiness, the kind that bears fruit behind the scenes in utter dedication to his religious brethren and in the composition of legislation and constitutions. In that sense the mobile, growing body of Dominicans during Agni's time may have identified more readily with Peter as a public-facing figure who was charged with high responsibilities by the papacy, and capitalized on that reputation in their presentation of their second canonized saint.

One of the most vexed questions about this text relates to its dating in relation to Jacopo da Varazze's *Golden Legend*. We know that the *terminus ad quem* for the composition of Agni's work is 1276, given the command of the General Chapter that convents procure a copy. According to recent research, we also know that the *Legenda aurea* was compiled in two stages. Jacopo wrote a shorter version at some point during the period between 1263 and 1266. A later, much augmented version appeared between 1272 and 1276 from Bologna. It was this later edition which became exceptionally popular, able to be found in hundreds of manuscripts and incunabulae.[17] Conversely Thomas Agni's effort is extant only in about ten manuscripts, never having enjoyed an early printed version, except for the heavily edited

---

[16] Though the *Vita Sancti Petri Martiris* contains many miracles stories, also the staple of "popular" saints' lives, nonetheless these were also favored in religious houses as well, both as material for meditation and for preaching exempla. The *Vitas fratrum* clearly demonstrates this. There was no bifurcation, or two-tiered religious model inside and outside the convent.

[17] Indeed there are later editions, dating from Jacopo's time as Archbishop of Genoa into the 1290s, however these are not widely diffused. See Giovanni Paolo Maggioni, "Ricerche sulla composizione e sulla trasmissione della Legenda aurea", *Biblioteca di Medioevo latino* 8 (Spoleto, Centro Italiano di Studi sull'Alto Medioevo 1995).

edition found in the Acta Sanctorum. In terms of the *Vita's* date of composition, I think the most likely time during Thomas' career that he would have had time to work on it was his stint as papal vicar of the city of Rome from 1264–1267. This would have also given him access to the papal archives, since he shows clear familiarity with the *Inquisitio in partibus* miracles prepared for the canonization. Before that time he was not well known, or was busy in the Holy Land. Later he was elevated to the position of a territorial Archbishop, the demands of which office would certainly have compromised his ability to write much. I consider that his last five years as Patriarch of Jerusalem are to be excluded entirely because of his evident political activity and long distance from any of the sources of Peter's life. We know that many miracles from the *Vita Sancti Petri Martisis* are also found in the *Golden Legend*, though the latest dated one is from 1259. I think it most likely then that Agni composed the work in the mid to late 1260s.

There are two sets of opinions about dependence. In the first place, Antoine Dondaine was convinced that Agni is merely a copy and elaboration of the canonization Bull and the *Golden Legend*.[18] Dondaine was arguing against the position of J. Zuidweg, who asserted Thomas Agni's priority based on his notable originality and clear access to much more source material than Jacopo, who was far more a compiler than an original author.[19] I agreed with Zuidweg in my 2008 study of St. Peter of Verona, though I had mistaken Toulouse MS 481 for a more original copy of Agni than it really was (an error corrected by the present effort).[20] In any case my reasoning in that instance still stands; neither Dondaine nor Zuidweg made a conclusive case for priority. I was convinced that at least Thomas Agni had access to significantly more sources than Jacopo, and agreed wholeheartedly with Michael Goodich's speculation that Agni had

[18] Antoine Dondaine, "Saint Pierre Martyr", *Archivum Fratrum Praedicatorum* 23 (1953): 117–128.

[19] J.J.A. Zuidweg, *De Werkwijze van Jacobus de Voragine in de Legenda aurea* (Amsterdam: H. Hoogwerf, 1941).

[20] Prudlo, *The Martyred Inquisitor*, 177–180.

access to the now-lost *Inquisitio* that preceded Peter's canonization.[21]

However, I am persuaded, in light of the arguments of Giovanni Paolo Maggioni (who kindly looked over the present work) that, given the originality of Agni's writing, and in light of the dating of the two versions of the *Golden Legend* that he established, Agni has priority over Jacopo. Maggioni is of the opinion that the life of Peter in the *Golden Legend* version of 1263–1266 draws only from the bull of canonization, whereas in the more complete version Jacopo made in the mid-1270s, he had Thomas Agni to hand to complement and augment his own work. In light of my speculations on the dating of Agni, this seems to be the most likely conclusion.

Aside from this difficult question we can readily identify most of Agni's other sources. He clearly makes use of the bull of papal canonization, *Magnis et crebris* from 1253, though he is not as slavish in copying it as Jacopo is. This bull's florid language, added to its brief recounting of Peter's life and miracles, gives Agni a foundational skeleton on which to work. Further, he also makes significant use of the material about Peter in the *Vitas fratrum* of Gerald of Frachet, however he is very free in construing the stories contained therein, rarely content to copy any text directly from the source. Thomas is very familiar with the Dominican liturgy concerning Peter as well, and weaves in various allusions to the mass and the office of the saint. Most significant for this life however, is how many more stories and miracles are included compared to all the foregoing sources, including the *Legenda aurea*. More than that, the skeletal list of miracles in the Bull is greatly expanded with names, locations, and details that are absent in the more formulaic papal document. This new information, coupled with the deep level of detail contained within Agni's text, leads me to the conclusion that Agni had direct access to the *Inquisitio in partibus* that was accomplished in late 1252 and early 1253, which contained the full dossier of depositions required to advance a cause for canonization. These are most clearly evident in the pre-canonization miracles listed by Agni. This *inquisitio* is no longer

---

[21] Michael Goodich, *Vita Perfecta: The Ideal of Sainthood in the Thirteenth Century*, Monographien zur Geschichte des Mittelalters 25 (Stuttgart: Hiersemann, 1982), 151.

extant, and so Agni's life seems to be accessing material about Peter that even predates the bull itself.[22] Adding to this are the large number of post-canonization miracles that Agni has access to that are not reported in any other sources. In 1255 the General Chapter of Milan enjoined that reports of miracles accomplished by the intercession of Peter be forwarded to the prior of Sant'Eustorgio in Milan.[23] Apparently these filtered in from all over Christendom, from places as far away as Poland, Hungary, and Ireland. Thomas appears to have had access to them as well, and many unique wonders are recorded only in his *vita*. Here lies the real value of this life. Not content with the bare record of vague miracles reported in the Bull, or even the popular stories told in the *Legenda aurea*, Thomas Agni produced a stylistically superior retelling of the details of the saint's biography and miracles, with real theological depth and a plethora of new information originating in the very earliest sources possible. It is for these reasons that I have sought to untangle the cut-and-paste edition of Ambrogio Taegio, done around the year 1500, which is a jumble of sources, radically rearranged from their original form, of which Agni comprises only about 40%. Since Taegio's version was incorporated in its entirety in the Acta Sanctorum, I have judged it necessary to go back to the original manuscripts and try to present Thomas Agni's life of Peter of Verona as close to his original as possible.

---

[22] This material allegedly existed in the Archivio di Stato di Milano before the Second World War; however an aerial bombing in 1943 caused the loss of many documents. I have made a thorough search of the archive and, while I have uncovered interesting documents about the early growth of the cult, I was unable to locate the *inquisitio* itself.

[23] *Acta*, I, 76–77.

THE EDITION

Manuscripts and Printed Sources

Extant manuscripts of the Vita Sancti Petri Martiris

F   Florence, Biblioteca Nazionale Centrale, Conv. Soppr. J.VII.30. (ff. 122r–137v). Thomas Agni of Lentini, *Legenda b. Petri martyris*. Parchment. 15th century.

N   Nürnberg, Stadtbibliothek, Cent. III. 69. (ff. 2–22) Thomas Agni of Lentini, *Legenda s. Petri martyris*. Three parts bound together. Light leather cover with coating pattern and stamp of the Dominican cloister. Parchment. Two columns, Gothic bookhand continuous from one hand. 15th century, written before 1462. 33.5x25 cm. From the Dominican Cloister, Nürnberg.

P1   Paris, Bibliothèque Nationale 18309 (ff. 1–45v) *Vita et canonisatio s. Petri, de ordine Predicatorum*. Legendarium. From Convent of Saint Jacques. Vellum. 2 columns. Early 14th century.

P2   Paris, Bibliothèque Nationale 5377. *Composita per Fratrem Thomam Agni, Patriarcham Hierosolymitanum, vita sancti Petri Martyris, de ordine Fratrum Praedicatorum*. Parchment. Two columns. Ca. 1300.

P3   Paris, Bibliothèque Nationale 14845 (ff. 85–112v) *Vita et miracula b. Petri, ordinis Fratrum Predicatorum*. Parchment, 2 columns. Mid 15th century.

Ps   Pisa, Seminaro S. Catherina 24. (ff. 99r–117v) *Fr. Thomas de Lentini, Legenda sancti Petri martyris*. Legendarium. Parchment, 2 columns. Mid 15th century. 33x24.5 cm.

S   Siena, Biblioteca Comunale degli Intronati, K.VII.2. (70ra–100ra). Thomas Agni of Lentini, *Legenda beati*

Petri martyris. Vellum, late 13th – early 14th centuries. 29x21 cm. Leather boards, four studs in each plate, two closing clasps. From Convento di San Domenico, O.P. (Siena). The ms. is a composite legendary, made up of five sections (ff. 1–107, 108–157, 158–170, 171–178 and 179–183) joined together.

Tr   Trier, Stadtbibliothek 1140/443. *Vita Petri Martyris ordinis Praedicatorum* (ff. 73–104). Wooden cover in pigskin, ornamented brass buckle, closure missing. Parchment. 15th century. 24x16 cm. From Jesuit College, Trier; accession in 1799.

Ty   Troyes, Bibliothèque Municipale 401. *Legenda s. Petri Martyris*. (ff. 94–101, contains only the life, not the miracles). Leather cover. Parchment. Late 15th century. Two columns. 36x27cm. From the Abbey of Clairvaux.

W   Library, College of Wooster, OH. Thomas Agni of Lentini, *Legenda S. Petri Martyris* (ff. 1r–28r.) Vellum. Early 14th century. 24x17 cm. Written in Northern Italy. Illuminated initial. Italian wood cover.

Vernacular Manuscript

Nv   Biblioteca Comunale, Negroni 10bis. *Vita e martirio del s. Pietro Martire dell'Ordine Predicatorum*. Tuscan Dialect. 13th century. Ed. in S. Orlandi, *S. Pietro Martire da Verona, Leggenda di fr. Tommaso Agni da Lentini nel volgare trecentesco*. (Florence, 1952), 3–74.

Lost manuscripts

Acqui Terme   Cattedrale, *Legenda S. Petri Martyris* (ff. 9v–17v). 15th century
Bologna   Convento S. Domenico, 13th–14th centuries.
Milan   Santa Maria delle Grazie; one of the mss. used by Ambrogio Taegio.

Bernard Gui, Speculum Sanctorale

T   Toulouse, Bibliothèque Municipale 481 (ff. 34v–38).
         Speculum Sanctorale III (Martyres), "Cuius (S. Petri
         martyris) gesta et passionem scriptsit primitus ven.
         Patriarcha ierosolimitanus fr. Thomas de Lentino et
         Innocentius papa IV in litera canonizacionis eiusdem, ex
         quibus excepimus que sequntur." 2 columns. 1st quarter
         14th century, probably 1324. Vellum. Perhaps Gui's
         original, dedicated to John XXII. From the Dominican
         convent of Toulouse.

A   Lisbon, Biblioteca Nacional Alcobaça 448. *Speculum
         Sanctorale III (Martyres)*, "Cuius (S. Petri martyris) gesta
         et passionem scriptsit primitus ven. Patriarcha
         ierosolimitanus fr. Thomas de Lentino et Innocentius
         papa IV in litera canonizacionis eiusdem, ex quibus
         excepimus que sequntur." Mid-14th century. 38x27cm.
         Parchment. French provenance.

Gui's section on the Martyrs (which include his life of Peter of
Verona) can also be found in Avignon, Musée Calvet 296; Brno, Univ.
knihovna A 44; Prague, Metrop. Kap. G. xxiii. 2; Prague, Nardoni
Mus. XII. D. 4, XIII. B.10. Only the two noted above were consulted
for this edition

Later Editions

AA.ss   Acta Sanctorum, "De Petro Mart. Ord. Praedic." Ed.
         Daniel Papebroch (Antwerp: Iohannem Meursium,
         1675), April III, 679–719; uses Taegio's edition with
         little change.

P4   Paris, Bibliothèque Nationale, Rés. des Imprimés D-
         1740, *les Sermones de Guibert de Tournai* (Printed:
         Louvain : Johannes de Westphalia, [inter 1477 et 1483],
         GW 10925). From the Dominicans at Bois-le-Duc, Late
         15th – early 16th centuries.

Taeg   Rome, Archivum Generalium Ordinis Praedicatorum
              XIV.54. 18th century. Copy of Ambrogio Taegio's
              compilation (ca. 1500) edited in AA.ss.

Textual Decisions

This edition has consulted every surviving manuscript of the Life of
Peter of Verona by Thomas Agni. In addition I have noted where the
edition differs from the compilation of Taegio, included in its entirety
in the Acta Sanctorum. This will be useful for comparing that
standard printed source in the Acta Sanctorum with the original *Vita*.
Further I have also noted the discrepancies between the original life
and the life of Peter edited by Bernard Gui in his *Speculum Sanctorale*,
written about 1324. I have done this for several reasons. First Bernard
is very early, being written before most of the surviving exemplars of
Agni's work. Further he cites his efforts as if they were merely excerpts
from Thomas Agni's life though – as we will see – Bernard adds,
omits, stylizes, and changes Agni's text at will. I have cited differences
between the life and miracles from Gui's original Toulouse
manuscript, as well as the text on the life (not post-mortem miracles)
from the Lisbon manuscript. While this is not enough to establish
Gui's text on its own (as there are several more surviving manuscripts
of that section of the *Speculum*), I believe this represents a strong start
for such a project. In any case it is useful to see what Gui is doing
with texts so early in the transmission history. When older or
contemporary accounts exist of narratives in Agni, I include references
to these so that they may be found in those sources themselves (which
have, in turn, all been edited).

In terms of the remaining 10 manuscripts, they are all copies of
the original *vita* of Peter authored by Thomas Agni. They all contain
most of the same information, with the exception of Troyes (**Ty**),
which concludes at the death and canonization and does not append
postmortem miracles. Most manuscripts are prefaced with a prologue
taken from a sermon of Thomas Agni for Peter's feast day "Tres sunt
qui testimonium dant" (all with the exception of Wooster [**W**], which

goes right into the life).[24] Siena (**S**) includes this prologue, but only added in the margin. Apparently the Sienese scribe preferred a different prologue from another sermon of Thomas Agni, entitled "Quis es iste qui venit de Edom". This prologue is only found in the Sienese manuscript, although Taegio saw fit to include it in his compilation, indicating Siena (**S**), or a lost related manuscript, as one of the textual sources for his work.[25] For the most part, with only a few exceptions noted in the edition, the copies all report the same narratives. In addition, there is an interesting vernacular translation from the mid-fourteenth century, undertaken in the Tuscan dialect. It has been edited previously.[26] No other vulgarizations of Agni seem to have survived (though there are many of the *Golden Legend*).[27] I have used this version to compare readings, seeing it as an early witness, but sometimes it could not aid in terms of word order or vocabulary selection because of its vernacular nature. It has also proven useful for Italian place and proper names, and I have usually deferred to it in those cases.

The transmission of the work in manuscript is, in broad outline, clear. Yet, although it is possible to establish a stemma with two clear families that descend from their respective sub-archetypes, actual relationships between manuscripts are, due to an unsurprisingly high degree of contamination, difficult to disentangle. Complicating the matter even further is the seemingly gradual assembly of the work, such that stemmatic relationships change during the post-mortem

---

[24] The first prologue can be found in its entirety in the sermon collection in Florence, BNCF Conv. Soppr. G VII 1464, fol. 18ra.

[25] The second prologue is also located in a book of Agni's sermons in Vatican, BAV Lat. 4691, fols. 69r-73v.

[26] S. Orlandi, O.P., *S. Pietro Martire da Verona, Leggenda di fr. Tommaso Agni da Lentini nel volgare trecentesco* (Florence, 1952).

[27] In fact, when originally published in 1862, the editor thought that it was a vulgar translation of the *Golden Legend*. R. de Visiani, *Vita e martirio del santo Pietro martire dell'Ordine de' Predicatori. Leggenda scritta nell'aureo secolo della lingua* (Verona: Tip. Vicentini e Franchini, 1862).

miracles, as texts were updated with accounts of new miracles and this process did not follow the original map of transmission.[28]

We may thus begin with the lower reaches of the stemma (see below, fig. 1), and the most distant family from the archetype, comprising **P1**, **P3**, **Tr** and **Ty**. Their common origins suggest a "French" tradition. The variants they have all inherited from their common sub-archetype (**Φ**) are numerous, comprising shared omissions,[29] additions,[30] misconstruals and errors,[31] use of synonyms or alternative

---

[28] For these comments on the stemma, I am deeply indebted to my friend and editor, Anthony Lappin, whose guidance was invaluable and who generously gave of his time.

[29] Twenty-nine in all, present throughout the work: II.ii.20 (om. "licet"), II.v.8 (om. "sui"), II.ii.6–7 (om. "ludicus predicator exurgit"), II.xiv.5 (om. "et uere"), II.xvi.15 (om. "precipue"), II.xvii.18 (om. "partis"), II.xx.2 (om. "et"), II.xxii.15 (om. "alia"), IV.ii.7 (om. "fieri"), IV.iv.4 (om. "diuinitus"), IV.xv.6 (om. "saltem"), IV.xv.15 (om. "porrigi"), IV.xvi.8 (om. "sub capa"), V.iv (title: om. cuiusdam), V.iv.4 (om. "nequaquam"), VI.ii (title: om. "integro"), VI.ii.3 (om. "serie"), VII.i (title: om. "et curato", with N), VII.iii.2 (om. "fratrum"), VII.v.5 (om. "deuote"), VII.v.9 (om. "quem socium"), VIII.vi.7 (om. "puer"), VIII.viii.2 (om. "ut potuit"), VIII.ix (title, om. "per totum"), VIII.x.12 ("hoc", against "in"), VIII.xi.14 (om. "predictum"), IX.ii, iii (om. part of title), IX.xv.4 (om. "martyri").

[30] Fourteen in total, spead throughout the work: II.vii.5 (add "factus" after "sanctus"), II.v.10 (add "hominibus" before "omnibus"), II.xii. 6 (add "contra"), II.xiv.6 (add. "in"), II.xix.3 (add "exinde sibi"), III.i.8 (add "in"), IV.vii.8 (add "reuocabat"), IV.ii.2 (add "iacoba"), IV.xvi.1 (add. "purgatione et" before "curatione"), VII.ii.13 (add "dicentes"), VII.vii.1 (add "autem"), VIII.i.1 (add "hec"), VIII.ii.9 (add. "hoc"), IX.xiii.7 (add "portauit uel").

[31] Some twelve in total: II.x.1 ("cotidie", against "taliter"), II.xviii.3 ("oppresserat" against "compresserat"), II.xviii.9 ("sub", against "suo"), II.xx.1 ("Cum" against "Dum"), II.xxii.5 ("in ore", against "mors" – a misreading), III.iii.6 ("ne", against "non"), VIII.iii.16 (the questionable "se transisserat" against "se conferat"), .iii.15 ("fratrum", against "factum"), VI.i.10 ("nunciata", against "insinuata"), VI.i.12 ("prius", against "post"), VII.v.1 ("fuit" against "Uir"), IX.ii.3 ("nichil ... nichil", against "ut ... uel").

forms,[32] and finally a large number of transpositions.[33] Whilst the descent from **Φ** is evident, given the sheer number of shared variants, establishing exact relations within the family is a rather fraught process. The closest manuscripts to each other in this group are **P1** and **P3**, who have a high number of shared readings, offering roughly

---

[32] II.i.15 ("coinquinabitur", against "inquinabitur"), II.iv.4 ("defuerunt" against "defuere"), II.xi.3 ("eius", against "ipsius"), II.xv.3 ("plura", against "multa"), II.xvii.6–7 ("linguosus", against "garrulus"), III.iii.7 ("mediolanum", against "mediolani"), III.v.19 ("in", against "ex"), III.iv.5 ("pro christi pugile", against "per christi pugilem"), III.vii.13 ("potuerunt" against "ualuerunt"), III.viii.3 ("gloriosa", against "gloriosum"), IV.vii.6 ("pro" against "ab"), IV.iv.14 ("sic" against "sicut [TA]/sicut utrobique"), IV.vii.8 ("ianua", against "ianuis"), IV.viii.6 ("exsurrexit" against "resurrexit"), IV.xv.5 ("haberetur" against "fieret"), IV.xvi.18 ("magno", against "multo"), IV.xvii.7 ("inquiunt", against "dicentes"), V.ii.10 ("aduentum" against "euentum"), V.iv.1 ("mediolanum", against "mediolanenses"), V.iv.3 ("nec", against "et"), VI.i.15 ("pre gaudio", against "per leticia"), VII.i.3 ("relatione ad nostram memoriam", against "attestatione ad nostram notitiam"), VII.ii.1 ("scripta", against "dicta"), VII.ii.4,12 ("raba", against "roba"), VII.ii.9 ("ardentem", against "accensam"), VII.ii.25 ("permanens", against "remanens"), VII.v.2 ("qui", against "nam"), VII.v.5 ("affluente" against "effluente", with **N**), VII.v.7 ("fuerit", against "affuerit"), VII.v.13,13 ("beati", against "sancti"), VIII.iii.12 ("eius", against "suum"), VIII.x.15 ("detrahimus", against "detraximus"), VIII.xi.3 ("quomodo", against "modo qualiter"), VIII.xi.4 ("quibusdam", against "cum aliquibus"), VIII.xi.4 ("dixerunt", against "condixerunt"), IX.iv.4 ("cibi" against "cibum"), IX.iii.3 ("terribile", against "(h)orribilis"), IX.xiii.4 ("Quod", against "que"), IX.ii.2 ("et", against "ac"), IX.iii.3 ("esset", against "foret"). Note also II.xx.3 ("specialis" against "speciali", with **N**), IV.iii.6 ("esset", against "essent"), IV.xvi.4 ("geralda", against "gerolda").

[33] Forty-one in total: II.viii.1–2, II.viii.6, II.viii.8, II.x.3–4, II.xv.4–5, II.xv.12, II.xvi.7 (with N), II.xvi.17, II.xvi.23–24 (with Ps), II.xvii.6–7, II.xx.4, II.xxii.6, II.xxii.14, III.iii.13, III.iv.17, III.v.5, III.vii.14–15, IV.ii.7, IV.iv.6, IV.v.4, IV.vii.1, IV.xv.16–17, IV.xvi.17, IV.xvii.7, V.iii.3–4, VI.i.13–14, VI.i.15–16, VI.ii.2–3, VI.ii.7, VII.iv.3, VII.vi.10–11, VII.vii.6–7, VIII.iii.7, VIII.iii.19,23, VIII.x.13, VIII.xi.10, IX.ii.1, IX.ii.3, IX.iii.2–3, IX.iii.6.

a third of all the variants within the "French" family of manuscripts.[34] Nevertheless, roughly a fifth of the familial variants are between **P3** and **Tr**.[35] The picture thus created is one of some contamination in transmission affecting **P1**, combined with the evident difficulty experienced by the scribes in deciphering their models, a difficulty transmitted from sub-archetype to its copy.[36] We may thus conclude, rather tentatively, that the "French" family is composed of a number of sub-sub-archetypes: **Φ**, from which descends **Ty** and **Φ2**; the latter, **Φ2**, from which descends **Tr** and **Φ3**; the latter, **Φ3**, from which descends **P3** and, via a sub-archetype (**Φ4**) contaminated with readings from higher up the stemma, **P1**.[37] Due to the prevelance of singular readings, none of the manuscripts may be said to be in the direct line of transmission.

---

[34] Omissions: IV.iii.6 (om. "frater"), IV.xi.5 (om. "fore"), V.iii.6 (om. "frater"). Additions: IV.xvii.13 (add "tales"; cp. add "taliter" Tr), VII.ii.12 (add "hoc"). Synonyms: IV.xvi.4 ("ualle sanata", against "ualle sana"), VII.xii.3 ("palmas", against "palmam"), VIII.xii.3 ("hereret", against "inheseret"). Misconstruals: II.x.1 ("continuabat", against "concinabat"), VII.iv.1 ("cortirugo", for "cortinago"), VII.x.3 ("alissecus", rather than "algisestus"), and VII.xi.1 ("saldaninus", instead of "soldaninus"). A number of joint omissions are found in sections which are wholly omitted by **Tr**: VIII.iv.6 (om. "super"), IX.iv.10 (om. "impediente tumore"), IX.vi.1 (om. "domina"), IX.x.2 (om. "aliis"). (**Tr** omits VIII.4,7,9,11; IX.4–10).

[35] Addition: III.iii.13 ("pedes"); slight alteration: VIII.xi.9 ("referretur", against "deferretur"), VIII.xiii.13 ("perlegit", against "legit"); transposition: VIII.x.7–8. Some variants are also echoed by a similar, although not identical reading in **P1**: thus at II.xiii.1, "qui" is omitted by P1 P3 Tr, but only P3 and Tr add "cum"; at IV.xvi.2, **P3** and **Tr** both offer "sanitas" (against "sanatio"), whereas **P1** offers "sanitatem"; VII.ii.13, all three manuscripts add "dicentes", but **P3** and **Tr** agree on the relative position of the word (**P1**, after "demones"; P3 Tr, after "responderunt"); the alternative reading at VIII.x.3 is the smallest imaginable (against "traiectum", **P1** offers "tinitum", **P3 Tr** "tinctum").

[36] For example, the otherwise inexplicable variants for "uel" at VIII.x.1: "duoque" (**P3**), but "et duo" (**Tr**).

[37] For a possible vector of contamination, see below, n. 46.

Staying at much the same level in the stemma, another set of manuscripts may be seen to descend from another sub-archetype, and, again, these have an identifiable geographical origin. **F**, **Ps**, **N**, **S** and **W** all evidently descend from this single sub-archetype, which we may refer to as **Σ**;[38] the manuscripts all have an Italian origin. We may further identify a further sub-sub-archetype, **Σ2**, whence descend **F**, **Ps**, **S** and **W**.[39] This grouping my further be refined by positing a further intermediate copy, **Σ3**, as the sub-archetype for **Ps** and **W**.[40] Other variants suggest localized contamination, or even scribal correction.[41] Finally, it is also clear that the Novara translation (**N**) derives from this branch, and seems closest to **W**. (I have noted correspon-dences where relevant with the Novara manuscript throughout, although, for the reasons mentioned above, this edition does not use it as a basis.)

Coming closer to the archetype, two sets of witnesses stand above these family groups. Both offer their own difficulties. Perhaps unsurprisingly, Bernard Gui had access to a particularly good

---

38 Omissions: IV.iii.11 (om. "in"); IX.xiii.7 (om. "portauit uel"); IX.xvi.3 (om. "ei"); additions: IX.xvii.6 (add "et"); VIII.xv.7 (add "sibi"); transpositions: VIII.i.1, VIII.ii.12, III.iv.14 , III.iv.2; deployment of synonyms: III.ii.10 ("ac" for "et"), VIII.v.5 ("connectenda" for "annectenda"), IX.iii.3 ("(h)orribilis" for "terribile"), IX.xiii.4 ("que" for "Quod"); minor but consistent variation: II.xxi.2 ("a*s*erbus", against "a*c*erbus"), IV.iii.5 ("qui nam", against "qui*s* nam"), IV.xiii.5 ("potue*r*it", against "potuit"), IV.xiv.1 ("uir*i*dis", against "ui*n*dis"), VII.ii.22 ("fe*c*it", agtainst "fa*c*it"), VII.v.1 ("maza*t*i", against "maza*r*i"), VIII.i.1 ("o*b*mittenda", against "omittenda"), VIII.ii.9 ("fac*i*et", against "fac*er*et"), IX.vii.3 ("dedondouenolla", against "deudeuonella"), IX.xvi.1 ("Filio", against "Alio ... filio"), IX.xvii.1 ("*n*euimus", against "*e*nuimus").

39 Thus, omission: IV.iv.14 ("est"); and minor variation: III.ii.1 ("sa*n*sonis", for "sa*m*psonis"), IV.xiii.2 ("*d*uci" for "*add*uci"), and VIII.iv.4 ("*e*ruptus", for "*r*uptus").

40 The sub-archetype was marked by a certain number of omissions: II.xiii.9 ("diuini"), II.xviii.2 ("uiri nobilis domini"), III.viii.2 ("sancti"), IV.i.12 ("uerissime"), VIII.iii.18 ("fratrum").

41 For scribal correction, see the inversion of VII.ii-iv in F, N, Ps, W and Nv, but which has been righted in S.

manuscript. Nevertheless, his *Speculum sanctorale* is itself a separate work, which corresponds to the author's own stylistic preferences, may have shown a degree of authorial evolution, and may even have subsequently assisted the contamination of other parts of the stemma. The other key witness to the archeytpe is **P2**. Generally, we might say that Gui sides with **Φ**, whilst **P2** aligns with **Σ**.[42] Nevertheless, there are occasions where **P2** sides with **Φ** alone,[43] something which happens very rarely with Gui's **TA**.[44] With this in mind, then, we may say that Gui's work descends directly or very closely from the archetype and offers a separate branch of the stemma. **T** and **A** both descend independently from a common sub-archetype.[45] **P2**, by contrast, descends from a sub-archetype from which **Φ** and **Σ** also descend.

A tentative stemma of the *Vita Sancti Petri Martiris* would thus appear as in fig. 1. Nevertheless, there is some evidence to suggest that

---

[42] Thus, for example, the omission of "muliere" (**P2**, **F**, **S**, **Ps**, **W**) at VIII.ix.6, or "et" (**P2**, **Σ**, **Tr**); transpositions (**P2 Σ**, against **TA Φ**): II.xvi.6, 17, II.xx.13, III.i.10-11, III.ii.4, IV.i.8, IX.xvi.4, IX.iii.2–3; additions (**P2 Σ** when compared to **TA Φ**): II.xx.1 ("uero sic", against "uero"), III.i.3 ("dominus"; omitted), IV.iv.14 ("sicut utrobique" vs. "sic(ut)"), VIII.ix.14 ("introduxit ille autem euigilans", against "introduxit"), IX.xv.4 ("recommenatus martyri", against "recommendatus"); and sminor variation at III.ii.2 ("eis", against "sibi"), and VI.i.4, where "aggratulans" (**P2 Σ**) is found rather than "congratulans" (**TA Φ**). Less comprehensive is "deposita" (**P2 Σ2**) against "reposita" (**TA Φ N**) at II.viii.14.

[43] Omissions: VI.i.7 (om. "diligenter"), VI.i.20 ("eius"), VII.ii.13,22 ("uestra"); addition: VIII.x.17–18 ("ad *mulierem instantiam et* multorum sollempni", against "ad multorum sollempni"); transposition: VIII.xi.11, VIII.ii.13, VIII.xiii.4-5; minor variation: V.iii.5 ("essem", against "fuissem"), IX.xvi.5 ("utilis" against "itineris").

[44] II.x.3 (om. "celerius"). Further possible, but by no means likely, examples might be II.v.23 ("potissimus" (**T** only), against "potentissimus"), , II.xi.5 ("romaniolam", against "romagniolam"). The common omission of rubrics (II.v–xxii, III.iv–v, IV.i–iii, v) may be to other causes than direct influence.

[45] For example, in the two lines II.viii.2–3, **T** omits "tamen" whilst **A** subsequently omits "diuinis".

the stemmatic relations depicted there do not hold for the final
section of the work, which can be explained by a later distribution of
that section, which would have been copied into the various
sub-archetypes by a different path of transmission.[46]

<hr />

[46] This can most clearly be seen at IX.i.1, where "ether" (**P1 P3 Tr**) is the
undeniably correct reading, against the banalizing "etiam" of **P2 F N Ps S W**.
Gui's *Speculum sanctorale* is of no help here, as he draws Peter's miracles to a
close at VIII.vi, noting in his explicit to the work that many miracles he has not
included still remain "in predicto libello". Nevertheless, the work of updating
the miracle collections with the Irish events contained in book IX would provide
a suitable opportunity for cross-stemmatic contamination.

Vita Sancti Petri Martyris

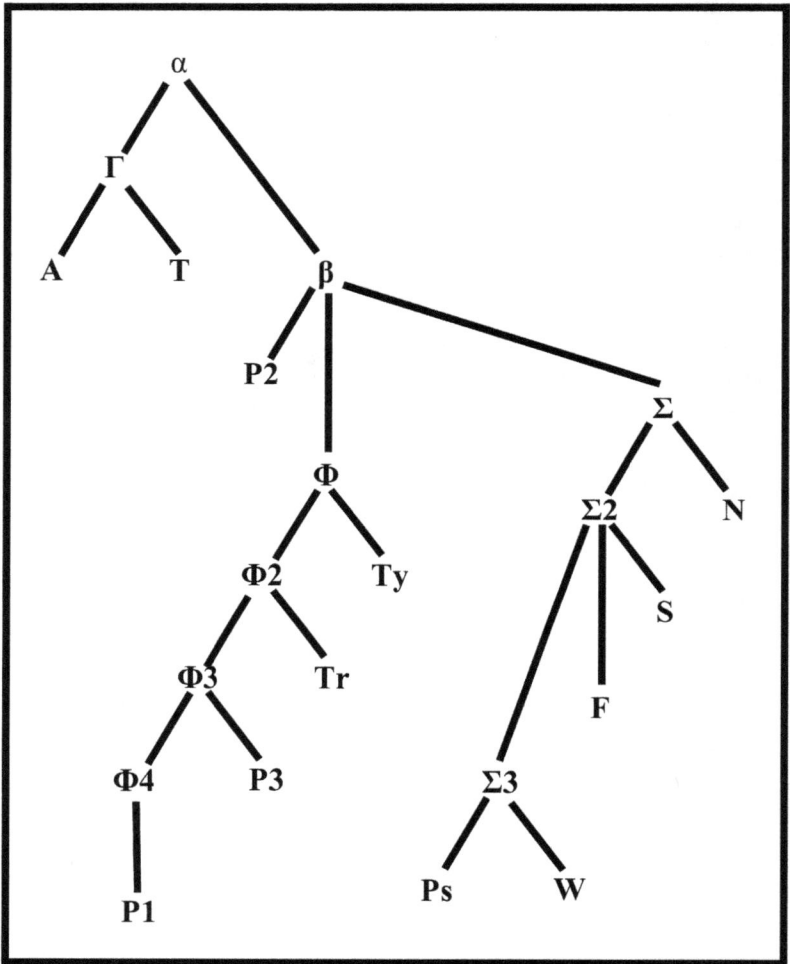

Fig. 1: Stemma to the *Vita Sancti Petri Martiris*

Based upon this stemma, this edition has tended to prioritize the Italian line **Σ**, along with **P2** as a crucially important witness, whilst at the same time maintaining an appreciation for Gui's text where it may be of assistance. I have preferred the readings from the **Σ** manuscripts because they are mostly earlier, seem to correspond with the Milanese text better, and because their variants often (but not always) make more sense. The translation is thus a product of the best reading that I could make of the remaining manuscripts, with a focus on **P2**. Very occasionally in the translation I have broken from the Latin punctuation, or relied upon readings in **Nv**, Taegio, or Gui, where they makes more sense or provide clarity.

In terms of the technical choices for this edition, I have kept the orthography and capitalization as close as possible to the medieval texts, and this includes punctuation: nothing has been regularized. I find it useful to present the reader something that closely resembles the original manuscript page. I have noted variants in all manuscripts, with the exception of obvious spelling issues, however I have noted where there are spelling differences in all proper names, place or personal, for these may be of interest both geographically and linguistically. I have not noted differences as to whether numbers are written out in Arabic or in Roman numeration, though if they differ in actual number I have noted it. On occasion I have broken up sections logically, even when there is no break in the manuscripts, but I always note in the apparatus where I do this. I have also noticed most error marks, expunxits, and marginal corrections, as these can help tell us about manuscript transmission and tradition. Thomas Agni's sources are noted throughout, in the notes of the edition, and in-line in the translation. Besides the critical apparatus, I also include an apparatus for sources, as well as a section that includes more general notes on the text.

LIST OF ABBREVIATIONS

Acta	*Acta Capitulorum Generalium Ordinis Praedicatorum*, Vol 1: 1220-1303, MOPH 3, ed. Benedict M. Reichert, O.P. (Rome: In domo generalitia, 1898)
AFP	*Archivum Fratrum Praedicatorum*
AGOP	Archivum Generalium Ordinis Praedicatorum, Santa Sabina, Rome
Antoninus	St. Antoninus of Florence, *Chronicon seu Opus historiarum*, Nuremberg: Koberger, 1484
BAV	Biblioteca Apostolica Vaticana
BHL	*Bibliotheca hagiographica latina* (Brussels: Bollandists, 1898) and *Bibliotheca hagiographica latina novum supplementum* (Brussels:Bollandists, 1986)
BNCF	Biblioteca Nazionale Centrale Firenze
BOP	*Bullarium Ordinis Fratrum Praedicatorum*, 7 vols., ed. T. Ripoll (Rome: Ex Typographia Hieronymi Mainardi, 1759)
LA	*Legenda aurea*, ed. Giovanni Paolo Maggioni (Firenze: Società internazionale per lo studio del medioevo latino, 1998). Vol 1
MOPH	Monumenta Ordinis Fratrum Praedicatorum Historica
PL	Patrologia Latina
SOP	*Scriptores Ordinis Praedicatorum medii aevi*, ed. Thomas Kaeppeli, O.P., 4 vols., (Rome: S. Sabina, 1970)
Surius	Laurentius Surius, *Historiae seu vitae sanctorum: juxta optimam coloniensem editionem*, (Augustae Taurinorum:

Ex typographia Pontificia et Archiepiscopali eq. P. Marietti, 1875), vol. IV, April.

Taegio   *Vita S[ancti] Petri Martyris Ordinis Praedicatorum*, ed. Ambrogio Taegio, O.P., Acta Sanctorum, 12 (Apr. III), 686–719

VF   Gérard de Frachet, O.P., *Vitae fratrum Ordinis Praedicatorum*, ed. Benedict Maria Reichert, O.P., MOPH 1 (Louvain: E. Charpentier & J. Schoonjans, 1896)

THOMAS AGNI DA LENTINI

VITA SANCTI PETRI MARTIRIS

THE LIFE OF ST PETER MARTYR

VITA SANCTI
PETRI MARTIRIS

I **Incipit prologus in uitam et passionem sancti petri martiris de ordine predicatorum**

Tres sunt qui testimonium dant in celo: pater. uerbum. et spiritus
sanctus. Et tres sunt qui testimonium dant in terra: spiritus. aqua. et
sanguis. Sanctorum gloriam multis et uariis testimoniis astruendam.
sapientia diuina prouidit. quibus corda fidelium attentius in laudem
5   sue bonitatis attolleret et in sanctorum uenerationem uehementius et
frequentius excitaret. Felix autem sanctus cui et celestia et terrestria
testimonia suffragantur: cui nec uirtus celestis desit ad gloriam. nec
laus terrestris ad famam longe lateque diffusam: et fidelium
testimoniis comprobatam. Que quidem in beato petro martyre. nouo
10 fidei pugile. clarius innotescunt. cuius sanctitati tota trinitas attestatur.
uidelicet patris potentia in miraculis. filii sapientia in doctrinis.
spiritus sancti gratia in uirtutibus et donis. quibus ipsum affluentius
decorauit. et pre participibus suis suorum carismatum unctione
perunxit. ut autem fides in fidei pugile contra impugnatores fidei
15 hereticos uidelicet amplius refulgeret. et suis refulgens radiis

---

I.i,1 Tres…I.i,3 sanguis] 1 Jn 5:7 (Johannine comma)

---

3 Incipit…4 predicatorum] Incipit prologus in legendam beati petri martiris ordinis
predicatorum compilatum per uenerabilem patrem fratrem Thomam de Lentino
patriarcham hierosolimitani. *F* Incipit uita sancti petri martiris de ordine fratrum
predicatorum composita per fratrem thomam patriarcham ierhosolimitanum *P2*
prologus] egenda *N* legendam *W* | in…passionem] *om. N W* | sancti] beati *Tr*
de…4 predicatorum] *om. W* continues directly to "et de eius ortu et puericia"
(I.ii,36–37)   **4** ordine] *add.* fratrum *N* | predicatorum] *add.* in festo beati petri
martyris *Tr add.* prologus *N* **I.i,1** Tres…I.i,28 prologus] *om. W TA add. al. man.*
subscr. S   **3** sanguis] *add.* prologus *P2*   **4** sapientia … prouidit] diuina prouidit

THE LIFE OF SAINT PETER MARTYR

Here begins the prologue to the life and passion of Saint Peter Martyr of the Order of Preachers.

"There are three who give testimony in heaven, the Father, the Word, and the Holy Spirit, and there are three who give testimony on earth, the spirit, the water, and the blood."(1 Jn 5:7) Divine wisdom has foreseen the glory of the saints strengthened by many and varied witnesses, through which He might lift up the hearts of the faithful in the praise of His goodness and that He might stir up more strongly and frequently veneration of the saints. Happy also the saint to whom both heavenly and earthly witnesses lend their support, to whom is neither heavenly power lacking for glory, nor earthly praise for repute, diffused far and wide, having been clearly proven by the testimony of the faithful. These things became most plainly known for blessed Peter Martyr, as a new battler for the faith, to whose sanctity the whole Trinity bears witness; namely the power of the Father in miracles; the wisdom of the Son in teaching; and the grace of the Holy Spirit through the gifts and virtues with which he was richly adorned, and before all his fellows He anointed him with the unction of His graces. [He was anointed] so that the faith might be more fully reflected in her champions against her assailants, namely the heretics,

---

I.i,1 There...34 honor] Florence, BNCF, Conv. Soppr. G VII 1464, fol. 18ra: | Taegio, Prologue 1

---

sapientia *Ps* **8** famam] *add.* in *P2* **12** gratia] gratiam *Ps* | ipsum] *om. P3* **15** refulgens radiis] *trans. Tr*

inuidorum oculos uirtuosius excecaret. non defuerunt terrestria
testimonia. dum et aqua innocentie baptismalis quam ex matris utero
illibate retinuit. et spiritus sapientie salutaris: quam per ytaliam
gratiose diffudit. et sanguis triumphalis passionis quam pro fide christi
20   uictoriose sustinuit. multiplicis glorie sue preconiis attestantur. ut
sanctis uirginibus. doctoribus et martyribus coequalis esset in premio.
quorum merito se imitatorem precipuum comprobauit. Que ut
amplius pateant. a primordiis uite eius narrationis sumentes
exordium. usque ad triumphum passionis sue. stilum breuem sed
25   rudem producendum decreuimus. adicientes non nulla celitus ostensa
miracula. prout ad nos seriem ueritatis fide dignorum detulit
approbata relatio. ad gloriam et honorem illius qui gloria et honore
suum martyrem coronauit. Explicit prologus.

Item alius prologus

Quis est iste qui uenit de Edom tinctis uestibus de Bosra? iste
formosus in stola sua gradiens in multitudine uirtutis sue? Mirum in
modum mirantur angeli nouum regem. cum nouis insigniis regiis
penetrantem celestia. Quis, inquiunt, est iste tam mirabilis celo. tam
5   spectabilis mundo. tam terribilis inferno. ut in nomine ihesu omne
genu flectatur celestium terrestrium et infernorum? qui uenit de edon
tinctis uestibus de Bosra? etc. Cuncta in admirationem deducunt illius
speculatores magnitudinis. nihil de contingentibus omittentes. siue ea
que ad passionis tincturam uel que ad resurrectionis gloriam. uel que
10   ad magnificam ascensionis pertinent comitiuam: singula namque
plena sunt admirationis et laudis. sed omnia simul juncta

I.ii,**1** Quis…I.ii,2 sue] Is 63:1   **5** ut…6 infernorum] Php 2:10

---

17 matris] *add.* ex *P3 exp.*   **18** et…**19** diffudit] *om. Nv*   **19** gratiose] illibate *P1 P3*
Ty Tr   **28** coronauit. Explicit prologus.] cora *Ps* | Explicit prologus] *om. F*
29 Item…prologus] Alius prologus proponatur qui magis placuit *S om. P1 P2 P3*
TA F Ps W Ty Tr N Nv Taeg   I.ii,**1** Quis…I.ii,36 sanctorum] *om. P1 P2 P3 Ps Ty Tr*

and that his shining rays might more powerfully blind the eyes of the hateful. Earthly witnesses too were not lacking; the water of baptismal innocence, which he retained untainted from his mother's womb, and the spirit of saving wisdom, which he spread purely throughout Italy, and the triumphant blood of his passion, which he endured victoriously for the faith of Christ, [all these] testify for praise of his manifold glories, that he was coequal with the Holy Virgins, Doctors, and Martyrs in the merited reward, and of whom he preeminently proved himself the imitator. That his glories might redound more fully, we take up this work with a short introduction, telling his story from the first beginnings of his life, up to the triumph of his passion; but we have determined that underdeveloped things be made plain, adding some miracles revealed by heaven, exactly as the approved acts by those worthy of trust brought the order of truths to us, to the glory and honor of Him, who crowned His martyr with glory and honor.

Another prologue

"Who is this that comes from Edom, in crimsoned garments, from Bosra? This one arrayed in majesty, marching in the greatness of his strength?"(Is 63:1) Let the Angels wonder in awe: the new King with a new standard entering the heavenly courts, "Who," they ask, "is this; so marvelous to heaven, so astonishing to the world, so terrible to hell, that in His name all knees should bend in heaven, on earth, and in the depths (Php 2:10): "Who comes from Edom, in crimsoned garments from Bosra?" All are led to admiration as eyewitnesses of His magnificence, nothing concerning Him is omitted that pertains chiefly to the bloodiness of His passion or the glory of His resurrection, or to His magnificent ascension: in fact everyone is full of admiration and of praise, but likewise all together increase in

I.ii

I.ii,1 Who...2 Bosra] Vatican: BAV Lat. 4691, fols. 69rb-73va | Taegio, Prologue 2

N W Nv TA **3** regiis] *om. S* **5** ihesu] eius *Taeg* **6** edob] Edom *Taeg* **9** que²] *om.*
Taeg

admirationem adiciunt. et mirabiliora ipsis intelligentiis supernis occurrunt. Mirentur igitur homines, per modum angelicum; mirentur auditores et inapectores tante uirtutis. uel per speculum in enigmate:
15 nouum militem cum triumphalibus indiciis regis uestigia prosequentem. dum sic cruore tinctus. et uictoriosus describitur in ueste sanguinea. sic fructuosus doctrine gratia per quam magnam comitiuam fidelium quasi seminis sui manipulos secum tulit ad dominum: siue quos de errore ad fidem conuertit: siue de culpa in
20 iustitiam transtulit. siue de mundo ad religionem adduxit. Hec sunt triumphalia indicia noui pugilis omnibus seculis admiranda: et ab antiquis temporibus inaudita ut sic triplici laurea laureatus ascendat: martyrum uidelicet in effusione sanguinis pro fide christi. uirginum in illibata munditia mentis et corporis: et predicatorum in
25 disseminatione sapienti salutaris per quam multos conuertit in uiam salutis. hec sunt que miratur celum ueneratur mundus et expauescit infernalis demonum et hereticorum exercitus. sicut ex uariis et mirandis miraculis innotescit. proinde sicut noua indicia uberioris glorie celo intulit. sic noua gaudia plenioris gratie mundo reliquit. et
30 confutatis errorum sequacibus ad eius sequenda uestigia. fideles cunctos attentius excitauit. uerum ut gestorum eius principium. finis et medium memori commendetur. a primordiis sue originis. per sue conuersationis decursum. usque ad triumphalem titulum passionis et mortis. seriem narrationis describendam. assumpsimus: prout ad nos
35 approbata descriptio fide dignorum adduxit. ad honorem illius qui est principium et finis honor et gloria et corona sanctorum. De eius ortu et puericia

---

14 per…enigmate] 1 Cor 13:12

---

12 admirationem] mirationem *S*   14 inspectores] spectatores *Taeg* | uel] uelut *Taeg* | enigmate] enigmata *Taeg*   22 temporibus] seculis *Taeg*   24 illibata] alibata *with error marks under* a *S*   27 ex] et *S*   35 illius] ejus *Taeg*   36 sanctorum] *add.* explicit prologus *F* | De…37 puericia] *om.* P1 P3 Tr Ty TA   37 puericia] *add.* primum capitulum *N*

admiration, and went forth more astonished at His heavenly wisdom. Therefore let men marvel, in the manner of the angels; let the hearers and seers of such great power wonder, just as through a glass darkly (1 Cor 13:12), a new soldier triumphantly following the footsteps of the King, whose victory speaks eloquently in stained wounds and bloody clothes; so abundant was the grace of his teaching, by which a great company of the faithful, whom he took with him to the Lord like seeds in his hand, whether it be those he converted to the faith from error, or carried from sin to justification, or led from the world to the religious life. These are the triumphal emblems of the new fighter, to be admired by all the world, and unheard of by the ancients, that thus he might mount up to the triple laurel of laurels; martyr, by the shedding of his blood for Christ; virgin, in unspotted purity of mind and body; preacher, by the dissemination of salutary truth, through which he converted many to the way of salvation. These are the things at which heaven marvels, by which he is honored by the world, and through which the demons of hell and the armies of the heretics take fright, just as he is known by various and wonderful miracles: hence he obtained new proofs of more abundant glories in heaven; thus new joys bequeathed fuller graces to the world, and through the refutation of the followers of error into supporters of his banner, he diligently stirred up all the faithful. Certainly we will relate the beginning, middle, and end of his history; from his first origins, through the course of his conversion, up to the triumphal honor of his passion and death, we take up the sequence of the story just as it is set down for us in the approved account, guided by those worthy of trust, to His honor, who is beginning and end, honor and glory, and the crown of the saints.

II Incipit uita sancti petri martiris edita a domino patriarcha ierosolimis.

Beatus petrus martyr predicatorum decus ytalie speculum et fidei pugil egregius. de prouincia lombardie ciuitate uerona ex parentibus hereticis traxit originem. ut tanquam lux de tenebris. rosa de spinis. flos exortus de sensibus. tanto amplius refulgeret in mundo redoleret
5 in claustro. rutilaret in celo. quanto de parentibus per errorem excecatis lucidus predicator exurgit. et saucitatis mente corporeque corruptis. decus uirginale procedit. ac de spinis eterno incendio deputatis inclitus martyr ascendit. licet enim beatus petrus parentes suos haberet hereticos quorum eruditionibus informari. et filium
10 natura doceat et puerum necessitudo compellat. tamen sic se mundum ab eorum seruauit erroribus et immunem: quod nec blandiencium dolositate parentum nec montionum instancia. nec frequentia uerborum ad hereticorum consortia uel colloquia induci ualeret aliquatenus uel compelli. Uidebatur enim quod nondum
15 legerat iam intellexisse prouerbium. qui tangit picem coinquinabitur ab ea. et illud apostolicum documentum. et corrumpunt bonos mores colloquia praua. Quod enim natura hominibus animalibusque contribuit. ut homo serpentis. agnus lupi aspectum abhorreat: et inditam inimicitiam sentiat. hoc puerum bone indolis unctio celestis
20 edocuit. ut uenenosorum serpentium insidias fugeret: et lupos rapaces pellibus ouinis contectos inimicos agnosceret. ac eorum consortia deuitaret.

II.ii,**15** qui...16 ea] Sir 13:1   **16** corrumpunt...17 praua] 1 Cor 15:33
18 agnus...aspectum] Mt 7:15

II.i,**1** Incipit...2 ierosolimis] *om.* P2 F S P5 W N *add.* Sancti petri martiris de ordine predicatorum. iii. kalendas maii cuius gesta et passionem scripsit primitus uenerabilis patriarcha ierosolimitanus frater thomas de lentino. et innocentius papa quartus in littera canonizacionis eiusdem ex quibus excepimus que sequuntur. *TA* II.ii,**2** prouincia] prouingia *W* | parentibus] *add.* infectis labe *T* labe *A* **3** de¹] *add.* teb *P3 exp.* **4** exortus] exortibus *P3* ib *exp.* **6** lucidus...exurgit] *om.* P1 P3 Ty Tr exurgit] exurgiret *Ps* **9** suos] *om. Tr add. al. man sup.* | eruditionibus] eruditione *TA Taeg* | et ... natura] filium non *P3* **11** ab eorum] *om. Tr add. al. man. dex.*

The beginning of the life of Saint Peter Martyr, edited by the Lord Patriarch of Jerusalem.

Blessed Peter Martyr, the ornament of the order of Friars Preachers, II.ii
the wonder of Italy, and illustrious champion of the faith, was born to
heretical parents in the city of Verona in the province of Lombardy;
just as light from darkness, a rose from among thorns, a flower taken
from briars, that he might better gleam in the world, might shine
more greatly in the cloister, and might radiate most brilliantly in the
heavens. Though greatly blinded by his parents through error, a
shining preacher arose. From illness of mind and corruption of body,
virginal glory arises. From thorns pruned for eternal flames, a
celebrated martyr ascends. And although Blessed Peter had to be
formed by the teaching of his heretical parents, still nature could
teach and necessity could compel the boy. Yet he saved himself clean
and pure from their errors, because neither by deceitful flatteries, nor
by impending danger, nor in frequent exposure to or conversations
with the heretics was he able to be induced or compelled even a bit.
Already he seemed to have understood that proverb: "he who touches
tar will be stained by it" (Sir 13:1) and the Apostolic counsel that
"bad conversation perverts good morals." (1 Cor 15:33) For because
nature governs in man and animals, man abhors the sight of a serpent
and the lamb detests the sight of the wolf, so having been introduced
to them he learned to feel their enmity. Good character instructed
this boy by means of a heavenly anointing, so that he would shun
those poisonous serpents and wild wolves concealed in sheep's
clothing (Mt 7:15), so that he would discern his enemies and shun
their association.

II.ii,1 Blessed … II.ii,1 Preachers] LA 421; VF, 236; Taegio, 1.1.

---

14 Uidebatur] *add.* Iam intelligatur *Taeg* | Uidebatur … 22 deuitaret] *om. TA*
15 picem] parem *Ps corr. marg. dex.* | coinquinabitur] inquinabitur *P2 F S Ps W N*
Taeg **18** abhorreat] *add.* ut *Ps* **20** lupos] *add.* agnosceret *Tr* | rapaces] *add.* licet *P2*
F S Ps W N Taeg

Unde cum nondum annos puericie transegisset circa septennium
constitutus et a scolis rediret quibus erat traditus litteris imbuendus. a
patruo suo heretico magno dyaboli laqueo. quid nam in scolis
didicerat interrogatus: respondit se christiane fidei symbolum
5 didicisse. credo in deum patrem omnipotentem factorem celi et terre.
per ordinem prosecutus. a cuius professione cum dictus patruus
prefatum puerum quasi rudem pugilem auertere niteretur. ut non
deum sed dyabolum potius fateretur horum uisibilium creatorem.
auctoritatibus etiam additis ad sui fomentum erroris. cum esset
10 causidicus et infidelitatis patronus: nichil tamen a puero. potuit
obtinere affirmante constanter quod legerat et quod scriptum erat. se
uelle credere et fateri. Quod ille uenator dyaboli et magnus
animarum seductor ubi perpendit. totum quod gestum fuerat patri
retulit: et ut petrinum a scolis remoueret. modis omnibus persuasit.
15 Timeo enim ait ne cum petrinus bene fuerit eruditus: ad meretricem
illam se conferat. et sic fidem nostram destruat. magnus ecclesie hoc
est conuenticuli chatharorum futurus si uixerit persecutor. Hoc autem
a semetipso non dixit: sed tanquam alter cayphas beatum petrum
hereticorum perfidiam destructurum futurorum nescius prophetauit.
20 Sed quoniam non est consilium contra dominum: sicut nec apud
filium: sic nec apud patrem optinuit sermo eius. qui fratris monitis
assensum non prebuit. sperans filium ad suam sectam per
heresiarcham aliquem in posterum atranhendum. cum in
grammaticalibus fuerit eruditus.

II.iii,17 Hoc … 19 prophetauit] Jn 11:49–52

II.iii,1 Unde] *no break* P1 P2 P3 Ty Tr F S Ps N W Nv | puericie] *om.* P3   2 et] *om.*
F Taeg | imbuendus] *add.* et Tr   3 magno … laqueo] *om.* TA   4 didicerat]
didiscerat P1 exp. s | christiane fidei] *om.* TA | symbolum] sed symbolum fide T
5 factorem] creatorem TA   6 prosecutus] *om.* Ps   9 cum … 10 patronus] *om.* TA
12 et² … 13 seductor] *om.* TA   13 ubi] ut Tr | totum … patri] patri totum quod
gestum fuerat F Ps W N Taeg patri totum quod fuerat S add. al. man. dex. gestum
14 remoueret] *add.* mol P3 exp.   15 fuerit eruditus] *transp.* TA   16 conferat]
transisserat P1 P3 Tr Ty add. Taliter siquidem sanctam ecclesiam heretici nominant
blasphemando. TA | ecclesie] *add.* nostre TA   17 chatharorum] chatharorum]
hereticorum TA   20 Sed quoniam … qui fratris] Sed quia res fiebat fratris sui TA

Then, about the age of seven, when he was returning from the school II.iii
where he was receiving his first lessons accompanied by his heretical
uncle, a diabolical trap was set. His uncle asked what he learned in
school. He responded that he had learned the Symbol of Faith, "I
believe in God, the Father almighty, maker of heaven and earth," and
all in succession until it was completed. The uncle, incensed at this
profession like a clumsy fighter, sought to turn the boy. It was not
God, he claimed, but rather the devil who is confessed to be the
creator of these visible things. With heretical authorities he tried to
convince the boy of his error, since the uncle was a patron of
faithlessness. Nevertheless nothing was able to prevail upon the boy,
who constantly affirmed that what he read and what was written he
himself wanted to believe and to hold. That seductor of souls and tool
of the devil considered what had happened, and related every detail
carefully to his father. He attempted with all means at his disposal to
get the father to remove little Peter from school. He said, "For I fear
that as soon as little Peter will be better educated, he will make a
compact with that harlot the Roman Church, and in such a way he
will destroy our faith." And this he did not say for himself, but just
like a second Caiaphas unaware of the future, (Jn 11:49–52) he
prophesied that the perfidy of heretics would be destroyed by blessed
Peter. But because there is no counsel that can prevail against the will
of the Lord, his words had no effect on either father or son. His father
did not give heed to his brother's warning, hoping his son would be
attracted to his sect later on under the influence of some heresiarch,
after he was educated in grammar.

II.iii,1 Then … II.iii,1 seven] LA 421-422; VF, 236; Taegio, 1.2.

---

sicut … 21 filium] *om. F* | sicut…qui] pater ejus *Taeg* **21** optinuit …eius] sermo
eius profuit *N* | eius] *om. S* **22** suam] *om. P3* | suam sectam] *transp. P2* **23** cum]
add. foret *TA* **24** fuerit] *om. TA* | eruditus] *om. Ps add.* ii. *P1*

De adolescentia eius et studio et ingressu ordinis predicatorum

Ut igitur dei beneplacitum impleretur qui cogitationes dissipat malignorum puer domi annis puerilibus iam excursis. et hereticis a pueritia quodammodo superatis. missus est bononiam ad studendum. ubi licet esset ab hereticorum instantia elongatus. non defuere tamen
5   noua impugnationum genera. florem pudicitcie sue subripere decertantia. adolescentioris etatis insultibus assueta. Quis enim inter carnis illecebras mundi fallacias. hostis insidias. inter denique lasciuias et lubricas sodalium comitiuas integritatem mentis et corporis sufficeret custodire. Non est fragilitatis humane. sed hoc donum dei
10   est: et paucorum priuilegium. quinimmo attestante beato Jeronimo in carne preter carnem uiuere angelicum est non humanum. Qua propter ingeniosus adolescens qui fortius erat animam bonam: et ad corpus incoinquinatum. et cor immaculatum totis anelabat affectibus: bonitatem circa se diuine dispensationis agnoscens et stupens. sicut
15   longo post tempore coram quibusdam fratribus sue puritatis consciis est confessus. quod in uia tam lubrica lapsum castitatis euitare potuerit. aduertens etiam puer sanctus. non esse tutum cum scorpionibus habitare. uelut alter ioseph pallium relinquit in manu egyptie suo insidiante pudori: et ad religionis refugium confugiendum
20   deliberans. mundum cum flore decidenti. parentesque cum perimenti errori despiciens. mundus ipse fratrum predicatorum ordinem est ingressus. futurus predicator eximius oppugnator heresum. persecutor

---

II.iv,10 in…11 humanum] Pseudo-Jerome, *Epistola* IX. Ad Paulam et Eustochium: De assumptione beatae Mariae Virginis, PL 30, 126.

---

25 De…predicatorum] *om. P1 P2 P3 Ty Tr TA* | predicatorum] *add.* secundum capitulum *N* **II.iv,1** qui…2 malignorum] *om. TA* **2** excursis] excursus *P3* transactis *TA* | hereticis] heresis *A* **3** est] *om. P1* **4** defuere] deficere *Ps* defuerunt *P1 P3 Ty Tr* **6** adolescentioris] adholescentioris *T* | Quis…11 humanum] *om. TA* **12** fortius] fortiter *Ps* | erat] *om. A* **13** totis] *om. W* | anelabat] helabat *P2 Ps* hanelabat *S P3 Tr W* anhelabat *P1 Ty N* anhelans *Taeg* **14** se] *om. Tr add. al. man. sup.* **16** euitare] *add.* non *P3* | euitare…17 potuerit] *transp. TA* **17** etiam] etiam] itaque *T* usque *A* | puer sanctus] *transp. TA* **18** habitare] *add.* uel *P3 exp.* uelut…19 et] *om. TA* **19** refugium confugiendum] confugium *TA* **20** cum2] tam *P1* **21** ordinem] *om. TA* **22** eximius…persecutor] *om. P3*

On his youth, studies, and entrance into the Order of Preachers   II.iv

So that the gracious purpose of God – Who destroys the plans of evildoers – might be fulfilled, the boy's home years having been completed, and the heretics to a certain extent having been overcome from his youth, the boy was sent to Bologna for study. Although there he was removed from the importunings of heretics, nevertheless he did not lack new kinds of challenges that were fighting to steal the flower of his chastity (having been accustomed to those of a more youthful age at home). For who, in the midst of the allurements of the flesh, deceptions of the world, plots of enemies and hazardous company of companions, might be able to sufficiently protect the integrity of mind and body? It is not fragile humanity, but rather the gift of God, and only a small number of people are privileged to receive it. "Living in the body apart from the body, men are not Angels," says Jerome. (Pseudo-Jerome, Letter 9 to Paula and Eustochium) Wherefore on this account the clever boy, fortunate in having been given a good soul, and by means of an unsullied body and immaculate heart, expelled all his passions, and recognized and marveled at the goodness of the Divine plan around him, and he confessed his purity before certain brothers that, while on that slipperly path, he had been able to avoid any lapses in chastity. Furthermore, though living with scorpions the holy youth was not perverted. Like a second Joseph, he abandoned the company of those lying in ambush on account of his modesty and he went into the hand of the Egyptians, and he fled to the refuge of the religious life, by cutting off the world with the flower of his chastity. He despised his parents by destroying error, and he was received from the world into the Order of Preachers. He was about to become an

---

27 On … II.iv,12 God] Innocent IV, "Magnis et crebris" Canonization Bull; LA 422-423; Taegio, 1.5. **II.iv,4** youth … Bologna] Taegio 1.3.

sordium. et uiciorum potentissimus obiurgator. In quo quidem ordine
per paupertatis et humilitatis uestigia. beatum patrem dominicum
25   ducem uirginem uirgo sequens. magnum perfectionis apicem attigit.
semper de uirtute in uirtutem proficiens et procedens quasi lux
splendens usque ad perfectum diem.

de nouitiatu et abstinentia eius

In nouiciatu siquidem contra carnem nimio zelo succensus. ne seruus
delicate nutritus proteruiret in dominum. sic se ieiuniis et abstinentia
nimie austeritatis afflixit. sic se uigiliis honestatis in orationibus
macerauit: quod mensuram proprie fragilitatis excedens. fere ciuem
5   perdidit dum uincere querit hostem. Neruis namque ipsius ex nimia
exinanitione contractis. ita dentes eius fortiter sunt obstricti: quod uix
ad glutiendum aliquod sorbile quolibet instrumento poterant aperiri.
Misertus est autem eius uel potius populi sui deus. nec passus est os
illud beatum obserari diutius: quod in medio ecclesie sue totiens
10   fructuose disposuerat aperire. Restitutus uero pristine sanitati.
modum mutauit abstinentie: sed non propositum uel consuetudinem
abstinendi. Humane autem imbecillitatis experiencia compassionis
adiuncta uirtuti. ita in eo pietatis et parcitatis ordinauit affectum:
quod licet sibi parcus et austerus permanserit. aliorum tamen
15   necessitatibus indulgentior semper fuit. ad quod unum quod gessit
iam antiquus in ordine. sufficiat exempli gratia: proferre in medium.
Cum enim ex uberiori gratia diffusa in labiis suis. ad deuotionem
ipsius plurimorum corda dominus inflammasset. gauderentque
uehementius cum sibi mittere poterant aliqua exenia pietatis. sicut

---

II.v,9   in...ecclesie] Sir 15:5, also the Introit for the Common of Doctors
17 gratia...suis] Ps 44:3

---

23 potentissimus] potissimus *P1 P3 Ty Tr T*   **24** beatum] *add.* petrum *P3 exp.*
patrem] *om. T*   **27** diem] *add.* iii. *P1*   **28** de...eius] *om. P1 P3 Ty Tr TA* | eius]
add. tertium capitulum *N* iii c. *W* **II.v,2** delicate] delicatus *P3 us exp. corr.* delicate
3 nimie] *add.* superflue *S exp.*   **4** ciuem] nunc *P3*   **5** dum] *add.* hostem *Tr exp.*
6 sunt obstricti] *transp. P1 P2 P3 Ty Tr* | obstricti] obstructi *N*   **8** sui] *om. P1 P3 Ty
Tr* | deus] *add.* et *Ty Tr* | nec] et non *P3* | passus est] *transp. TA*   **9** illud beatum]

extraordinary preacher, a battler against heresy, a hater of uncleanness, and a most powerful prosecutor against sins. In that order, characterized by humility and poverty, and led by Father Dominic, he was a virgin following a virgin. He achieved the heights of great perfection, building from one virtue to another, going up like a wondrous light until his final day.

On his novitiate and his habit of abstinence II.v

During his novitiate he was set on fire with great zeal against the flesh, heedless that the delicate servant nourished in the Lord might be crushed. He afflicted himself with fastings and abstinences of excessive harshness, and weakened himself in prayer and by strenuous vigils. However, by exceeding the proper measure of his fragility, he nearly lost his life, which the enemy sought to destroy. His strength was ebbing from excessive weakness and his jaw was so strongly contracted that it was hardly able to be forcibly opened by an instrument in order to get him to swallow anything. The Lord, having pity on him or rather on His people, did not allow that blessed mouth to be sealed for a long time; in the midst of His Church He ordained it to be opened many times (Sir 15:5). Having had an experience of human weakness, he added compassion to his virtues, and he ordered the dispositions of goodness and moderation. Although he remained himself frugal and austere, nevertheless he was always indulgent towards the needs of others, as one who was already senior in the order. Let one example suffice, placed into the middle [of our narrative]. From the abundant grace poured forth on his lips (Ps 44:3) the Lord inflamed a great many hearts in devotion to him, so that they rejoiced exceedingly with him, and they were able to present many pious gifts (as the brethren who then were present

---

34 On...II.v,12 many] Innocent IV, "Magnis et crebris" Canonization Bull; LA 422-423; Taegio, 1.5. **II.v,1** his...he] Taegio, 1.4.

---

illius *TA*   **10** uero] igitur *TA*   **12** autem] *om. Tr*   **13** in...pietatis] pietatis in eo *TA*
16 antiquus] antiquos *TA*

20 fratres qui tunc aderant diligentius notauerunt. de omnibus cibariis
que ob sui gratiam cotidie mittebantur habunde. per unam
quadragesimam. aut nil comedit. aut modicum. sicut solitus erat
sepius abstinere. illum sequens. licet a longe petrus iste. cui uenit
ministrare non mininstrari quique pro nobis cum diues esset factus est
25 egenus ut illius inopia nos ditaret.

de munditia et perfectione eius

Porro intergritatem mentis et corporis sicut a primeuis incepit
temporibus. sic semper illibatam studuit conseruare. et in
conseruando proficere. ut uirgo corpore uirgo mente. nullius
umquam mortalis criminis contagium senserit. sicut suorum
5 confessorum fideli testimonium est probatum. Ne uero per ocii
desidiam hostilibus pateret insidiis. in iustificationibus domini
exercebatur assidue. ut eo circa uirtuosa totaliter occupato. nichil
uitiosum in ipso locum aliquatenus optineret. et a spiritualibus
nequitiis tutus esset. quantum insuper fuerit deuotione gratus.
10 obedientia placidus. benignitate suauis. patientia constans. caritate
prestabilis. et in cunctis morum maturitate compositus protestantur
diffusius seculares et fratres qui uiderunt. qui eius meruerunt
conforcium et sibi famuliarius adheserunt.

---

23 uenit ... **24** mininstrari] Mt 20:28

---

20 aderant] adherant *P1* | diligentius] diligenter *TA*   **22** nil] nihil *A* | sui] eius
TA | unam] *add.* totam *A*   **23** illum ... **25** ditaret] *om. TA*   **24** quique] quicque *P2*
25 ditaret] *add.* iiii *P1*   **26** de ... eius] *om. P1 P3 Ty Tr TA* | eius] *add.* quartum
capitulum *N* iiii. *W* **II.vi,1** a ... 2 temporibus] *om. Taeg*   **2** illibatam] illibata *A*
3 uirgo[1]] *add.* in *P1 Ty* | nullius] *add.* Unde in littera canonizationis eiusdem
Innocentius papa iiii prosequitur in hunc modum: Ipse namque ueritatis filius et
bonitatis alumpnus conuersatione conspicuus et opinione mirabilis miro prefulsisse
nitore munditie, uirginitatem integre custodisse nec mentis habuisse: nec corporis
corruptelam. et *TA*   **4** umquam] *om. TA* | contagium senserit] sensisse contactum
TA | sicut] firma *TA*   **5** fideli ... probatum] assercione monstratur *TA*   **6** hostilibus]
ostilibus *T* hostibus *P1* | in] et *A*   **7** eo] *add.* ca *P3 exp.* | uirtuosa] licita *TA* u *P3*
exp. | nichil ... 8 uitiosum] *om. TA*   **8** aliquatenus optineret] illicita non haberent
TA   **9** quantum ... fuerit] *om. TA* | deuotione] *add.* insuper *TA*   **10** suauis] *add.*

diligently recorded). On account of him they daily sent abundant provisions of food, although the whole of one Lent he ate nothing at all, or just a bit. He was in the habit of often abstaining, following Him – though far removed in time from that other Peter – who came to serve and not to be served, (Mt 20:28) Who, though rich, was made destitute for us so that His poverty might enrich us.

On his purity and perfection II.vi

He was always occupied with preserving the integrity of his mind and body, so that they would always be unsullied, and he accomplished this by maintaining his purity, so that by a virginal body and mind, he did not experience the contagion of any mortal sins at all, as the reliable testimony of his confessors has proven. He did not even permit himself the idleness of leisure, a trap of the enemy. He was regularly drilled in the right ways of the Lord, and was seized totally by virtue; nothing pertaining to vice could prevail in him, and he was protected from spiritual wickedness. He was pleasing in devotion, gentle in obedience, agreeable in kindness, constant in patience, preeminent in charity, and in ripeness of morals complete; as diverse laymen and brethren who saw him testified, who merited to have knowledge of him and who were most familiar with him.

---

28 On...II.vi,13 him[2]] Innocent IV, "Magnis et crebris" Canonization Bull; LA 422-423; Taegio, 1.5.

---

pietate compatiens *T* **11** prestabilis] prestabit *P3* | protestantur...13 adheserunt] alios profusis uirtutum aromatibus atrahebat. *TA* **12** uiderunt] *add.* habere *P3* qui[2]] *add.* et *N* **13** sibi] *om. Tr add.* al man. *sup.* | adheserunt] *add.* u *P1*

de humilitate eius

Porro quantumcumque polleret moribus et meritis prefulgeret. ne quasi puluerem iactaret in uentum. si sine humilitate uirtutes alias in cordis armario congessisset. Sic se humilem et subiectum in congregatione fratrum exhibuit ut ad fratrum obsequia in quibus sanctus iuuenis occupabatur interdum. se facilem et uoluntarium exhiberet. sepe namque pia sollicitudine seruiebat infirmis. frequenter hospites ylari recipiebat affatu. nonnunquam uero uerborum et gestuum compositione seruata discrete peragebat officium ianitoris: ad nulla officia quantumcumque humilia se difficilem exhibens uel inuitum.

de assiduitate studii eius precipue circa ea que erant fidei

Ceterum licet interdum cum martha exterioribus ministeriis sollicite inseruiret: tamen sedens ad pedes domini cum maria. non diebus neque noctibus a diuinis cessabat colloquiis euangelium christi uel aliquem sacrum codicem. sub ascella uel in pectore uel in manibus gerens. semper cum poterat uel lecta meditans. uel audita ruminans et memorie recommendans. Inerat enim ei ardens desiderium sapientie. et tantus amator factus est legis diuine: ut cum eunucho ethyopie etiam in ministerio cotidiano positus. sacras cum posset litteras legere non cessaret. Sic enim in ipso grata sibi uicissitudine succedebant. ardor discendi et desiderium promerendi: ut mirum in modum interdum non minoratus actu non minus percipere desistebat.

II.viii,7 eunucho ethyopie] Acts 8:26–40

---

14 de...eius] *om.* *P1 P3 Ty Tr TA* | eius] *add.* quintum capitulum *N* v. *W*
II.vii,2 iactaret] *om.* *P3* | alias] *om.* *A* **5** sanctus] *add.* factus *P1 P3 Ty Tr*
7 recipiebat] suscipiebat *A Taeg* | recipiebat affatu] *transp.* *P3* | affatu] affectu *A*
Taeg affe tu *W (includes space, betokening a certain scribal uncertainty)* | uero] *om.*
TA **9** difficilem] *add.* se *Tr exp.* **10** inuitum] *add.* vi *P1* **11** de...fidei] *om.* *P1 P3*
Ty Tr TA | precipue...fidei] *om.* *F* | fidei] *add.* sextum capitulum *N* vi. *W*
II.viii,1 sollicite...2 inseruiret] *transp.* *P1 P3 Ty Tr* **2** tamen] *om.* *T* | sedens] *om.*
P3 **3** diuinis] *om.* *A* **4** ascella] acella *P3* axilla *Taeg* | uel[1]...manibus] uel in

On his humility

But however strong one might be in virtues and however resplendent one might be in merit, still one will be scattered like dust before the wind if the other virtues are gathered in the heart's chamber without humility. He himself exhibited humility and submission in the midst of the congregation of Friars, and the holy youth occupied himself in their service often, with a willing and prompt heart. For instance, he often served the sick with tender solicitude, frequently he received guests with cheerful affection, sometimes he carried out the office of porter, watching with composure in words and gestures. In no work, however humble, did he show himself obstinate or reluctant.

On his care for study, especially regarding those things relevant to the Faith.

Sometimes like Martha, having looked after external things with careful attention, and then sitting at the feet of the Lord with Mary, neither day or night saw the cessation of his prayers and his Divine colloquies. He always carried the Gospels of Christ or another sacred text under his arm, or on his breast, or in his hands, always reading when he was able, or meditating on the reading, or thinking about something he heard and committing it to memory. For an ardent desire for wisdom animated him, and he was made a great lover of the Divine law, though, like the Ethiopian Eunuch, (Acts 8: 26–40) he was burdened by daily tasks, when he was free he never ceased to read. In this way he graciously matured in a love of speaking and the desire of doing well, so that, wonderfully, though now and then he had to perform routine daily tasks, he never ceased to learn. For

---

II.vii,1 But... II.vii,1 one] Taegio, 1.7. **II.viii,1** Sometimes... II.viii,18 Scriptures] Taegio, 1.7

---

manibus uel in pectore *Ps* **6** memorie] *add.* co *P3 exp.* | ei] *add. sup. P1 om. P3 Ty Tr* | sapientie] *add.* ei *P3 Ty Tr* **7** ethyopie] ethyope *P1* **8** litteras legere] *transp. P1 P3 Ty T* **9** cessaret] cessabat *TA* **10** promerendi] promorendi *T*

Contulerat enim ei diuina prouidentia cor docile. tenacem
memoriam. ad deposita custodienda fideliter. et linguam eruditam. ad
reposita efficaciter dispensanda. Unde sine more dispendio factum est
15   cor eius promptuarium sacre legis: et sanctarum armarium
scripturarum.

Per idem uero tirocinii sui tempus opprobriorum hereticorum ecclesie
dei exprobantium non immemor. neque obliuiosus zelator effectus:
sic animo suo fidem precipue. et ea que ad fidei pertinent
defensionem et heresum impugnationem impresserat: ut quasi fidei
5   propugnator ardentior totum in illius et contra hostes eius se
manciparet obsequium: quod queque ipsius uerba et studia uirtutem
fidei redolerent. ac sic circa defensionem ipsius fidei pro qua totus
ardebat preualuit et profecit. quod contra illius diros hostes
postmodum mente intrepida feruentique spiritu continuum certamen
10   exercens. suum tandem agonem diuturnum uictrici superante
martyrio feliciter consummauit. Pro hac enim a primeuis temporibus
mortem subire cupiens. hoc principaliter a domino attentis et crebris
supplicationibus postulasse probatur: quod non sineret eum ex hac
luce migrare nisi sumpto pro illa calice passionis. Nec fraudatus est
15   desiderio suo.

Ideoque disponente domino. lucernam suam quam taliter concinabat
non occultare sub modio: sed breui temporis spatio super

---

13 deposita] 1 Tm 6:20   **15** sanctarum…16 scripturarum] Eph 6:10–20
II.ix,14 Nec…15 suo] Mt 26:39   **II.x,2** non…modio] Mt 5:14-15; Mk 4:21-25;
Lk 8:16-18

---

12 enim ei] ei enim *P3* nim *exp. to read* ei | prouidentia] *add.* cor dolice *P3 exp.*
docile] docibile *Tr add.* et *P3 TA*   **14** reposita] deposita *P2 F S Ps W Taeg*
16 scripturarum] *only TA break here. All Agni sources continue through.*
II.ix,1 tempus] *add.* oppo *P3 exp.*   **2** effectus] *add.* seruens amator fidei cultor
precipuus propugnator ardentior. *TA* (*om.* precipuus *A*)   **3** suo…precipue] *om.*
TA | precipue] *add.* illam impresserat *TA* | pertinent] pertinet *A*   **4** heresum]
heresim *A* | impresserat] *om. TA* | quasi…5 ardentior] *om. TA add.* se *TA*   **5** se]
om. TA   **6** quod] et *TA* | queque] quaque *P3* | ipsius] *om. Ps add.* ua *Ps exp.*

Divine providence brought together in him a docile heart and a steadfast memory for loyally protecting the deposit of faith (1 Tm 6:20), and a learned tongue for effectively dispensing that same deposit. Whence without delay his heart was made a repository for the Sacred Law and the holy armor of the Scriptures. (Eph 6:10–20) From the time of his youth, he had neither been heedless nor forgetful of the reproach of the heretics, blasphemers of Holy Church, and he had been made zealous, so that his soul was especially prepared for the defense of the faith and for those things that could combat the attacks of the heretics, so that – like a fiery champion of the faith – he might give himself over to Her service against Her enemies. Whether in his words or his studies, he gave off the sweet aroma of the truth of the faith. He was on fire for the defense of that faith, and he prevailed and perfected everything by waging incessant combat against those horrible enemies with a fearless mind and fervent spirit, and in the end he happily consummated his long struggle by attaining the victory of martyrdom. For he wished to endure death from an early age, this desire manifested itself in being submissive to the Divine Will and by making frequent supplications to the Lord, that he might not be permitted to pass from this life, without drinking from the chalice of suffering (Mt 26:39). He was not cheated of his desire.

For that reason, since the Lord set in order his lamp, which he made in such a way as not to hide it beneath a bushel, (Mt 5:14–15; Mk

II.ix

II.x

II.ix,1 From … II.ix,1 youth] Taegio, 1.8. **II.x,1** For … II.x,7 general] Taegio, 1.9.

---

studia] opera *T* | uirtutem] ueritatem *A Taeg* **8** illius] *add.* hereses *Tr exp.* **9** mente … continuum] *om. F* | certamen … 10 diuturnum] *om. S add. al. man. dex.* **11** primeuis temporibus] *om. TA* **13** non] *om. P3* **14** nisi sumpto] *om. P2 add. al. man. sup.* nisi | illa] illo *A Taeg* illo *Ps exp. add.* nisi sumpto *P3* nisi *exp.* | Nec … 15 suo] *om. TA* **15** suo] *only TA break here. All Agni sources append II.x directly.* **II.x,1** quam] quamque *P2* | quam … concinabat] *om. TA* | taliter] cotidie *P1 P3 Ty Tr* | concinabat] continuabat *P1 P3 N* concremabat *Taeg* **2** breui … spatio] *om. TA*

predicationis candelabrum altius sublimare. credita est sibi celerius
eloquiorum dispensatio diuinorum: et celesti uirtute suum studium
5   comitante: et predicator factus est generalis.

de predicatione eius et deuotione populi ad eum

Ubi uero uelut alter gedeon tubam predicationis assumpsit: quam
glorioso clangore sonuerit. hostes fugans fideles excitans: in multis
partibus est auditum. Exiuit enim sonus ipsius in omnem terram
prouincie lombardie. apud urbem etiam et non per modicam partem
5   tuscie: per totam romagniolam. et per marchiam anchonitanam. Quas
enim ciuitates aut oppida ibi sita deuotis aliquando clamoribus non
impleuit? Quarum gentium per dicta loca morantium. non concussit
corda uel pulsauit auditum? ubique inmemoratis partibus: sancte
opinionis ipsius diffusus est odor. aliis odor uite in uitam. aliis odor
10   mortis in mortem. ubique est reddita persona spectabilis ubique
factum est celebre nomen eius: auris audiens beatificabat eum. et
oculus uidens ei de sanctis operibus. de exaltatione quoque fidei et
uictoriosa confutatione erroris testimonium perhibebat. Quantos
autem aut quales fructus fecerit in salutem animarum uel in
15   suorum copia meritorum? solus nouit qui multitudinem stellarum
enumerat. cui nuda sunt omnia et aperta. Uerumptamen ex
diuturnitate temporis. ex multiplicitate laboris ex magnitudine
gratie et uirtutis. preclara beati petri merita clarius innotescunt. Si
enim beatus est qui iugum domini ab adolescentia sua portauerit?

II.xi,2 in … 3 auditum] Jdg 6–8   **13** confutatione … perhibebat] Mt 13:16
19 qui … portauerit] Jer 2:20

---

3 sibi] illi *F* | celerius] *om. P1 P3 Ty Tr F TA*   **4** eloquiorum dispensatio] *transp. F
TA* | diuinorum] *add.* celerius *P1 P3 Ty Tr*   **5** et] *om. F S Ps P2 Tr N W* | et …
generalis] factus est predicator generalis *F* | factus] effectus *TA*   **6** de … eum] *om.
P1 Tr TA* | eum] *add.* vii capitulum *N* vii. *W*   **II.xi,1** Ubi] *add.* uult *P3 exp.*
2 fugans] *om. F* , *add.* ac *FA*   **3** ipsius] eius *P1 P3 Ty Tr*   **4** urbem] urbes *P1*
etiam] christi *Tr om. T add. marg. sin. P1* | et] *om. S* | non per] *transp. F S Ps N
W*   **5** tuscie] *add.* et *F* | totam] *om. A* | romagniolam] romaniolam *P1 P2 Tr TA*

4:21–25; Lk 8:16–18) but to raise up within a brief space of time all the higher on the lamp-stand of his preaching; the dispensation of the divine word was entrusted to him all the more swiftly, with the heavenly power accompanying his zeal, and he was made a preacher general.

On his preaching and the people's devotion to him   II.xi

To be sure, wherever he took up the trumpet of preaching he was like another Gideon, he sounded like some glorious blast, stirring up the faithful and putting his enemies to flight, and he was heard in many different places. (Jdg 6–8) For his sound went forth in all the lands of the province of Lombardy, even up to Rome, and through a great part of Tuscany, and among the whole of Romagna and the Marches of Ancona. For what city or village was not stirred to devotion by his shouts? What people were there, when he stayed in those places, whose hearts he did not rouse or whose ears he did not smite? In new regions the odor of heavenly doctrine was everywhere diffused, to some it was an odor that led to life, to others it was an odor that led to death: everywhere he has become a marvel, everywhere his name is made famous. The ear that heard him blessed him, and the eye which saw him bore witness about him regarding the accomplishment of good works, the exaltation of the faith, and the victorious confutation of error. (Mt 13:16) How much and what kind of fruit he bore in the salvation of souls and in his abundance of merits is known only to Him who can count the multitude of the stars, to whom everything is bare and laid open. But still, over a long period of time, from a multitude of labors, and from a bounty of grace and virtue, the splendid merits of Blessed Peter became plainly known. For if he is

---

Quas…8 auditum] *om. TA*   **7** impleuit] excitauit *Taeg*   **8** ubique…10 mortem] *om. Ty*   **9** ipsius] *F S Ps* | aliis[1]…10 mortem] *om. TA*   **10** spectabilis] exspectabilis *P3 TA* prestabilis *N*   **12** de[2]…13 uictoriosa] et exaltatione fidei et *TA*   **13** Quantos…18 innotescunt] *om. TA*   **16** Uerumptamen…18 innotescunt] *om. Taeg*

20   quanto beatior qui tamquam beniamin adolescentulus. in excessu
sanctitatis et uirginitatis thalamo. triginta fere annorum spatio in
predicatorum collegio comoratus. totum tempus et numerum
dierum uite sue studiose in obsequiis diuinis expendit. usque ad
triumphalem titulum passionis. Si autem bonorum laborum gloriosus
25   est fructus; quis labores quos operarius domini pertulit. siue in
confessionum fastidiis. siue in predicationum clamoribus digne
poterit enarrare.

    Ut enim dies pleni inuenientur in eo. et noctes uacuas non haberet.
nocturna silentia humane deputata quieti. post dormitionem breuem
decurrebat in studiis lectionum. et sompni tempus deuotis orationum
suspiriis occupabat. Dies autem impendebat commodis animarum.
5   uel cotidianis et sedulis imminendo predicationibus. uel confessionum audientie insistendo. aut hereticum dogma pestiferum ualidis
rationibus confutando: in quibus specialis dono gratie noscitur
claruisse. Sic uero gratiam grate dominus exequauit. quod multitudo
populi ad predicationem eius undique confluentis: gratie ipsius
10   magnitudinem ostendebat De ciuitatibus enim et castris. cum uexillis
et tubis sonantibus erumpebant obuiam uenienti: recedentem quoque
tot aliquando sequebantur. quod uix ab eis se poterat separare. Sepius
etiam ubi predicare statuerat. innumerus turbarum concursus loca
preripiens et tempus perueniens. ipsum intolerabiliter opprimebat.
15   propter quod mediolanensis populus in insigne deuotionis indicium
in carruca ex pictis asseribus fabricata. non collis animalium sed
humeris uecta fidelium. collocatum sanctum. et a pressura

---

20 beniamin adolescentulus] Gn 49:27   **24** bonorum…25 fructus] Wis 3:15.
II.xii,1 dies…eo] Ps 72:10

---

20 adolescentulus] *add. Ipse enim tanquam beniamin adolescentulus ad adolescentia
sua TA*   **21** annorum] anno *T*   **22** et…23 studiose] uite sue *TA*   **24** Si…27
enarrare] *om. TA Taeg* | bonorum] bonorum operum uel *P1 Ty* bonorum operum
Tr operum *P3*   **25** pertulit] *om. Ps* | in…26 siue] *om. P3 add. al. man.* in
confessionum fastidiis siue   **27** enarrare] no break *P1 P2 P3 Ty Tr S F Ps N W Nv*
II.xii,1 enim] in eis *P3 exp.* | haberet] *add.* et *Ps*   **3** deuotis] *add.* interdum *S*
orationum…4 suspiriis] orationibus *A*   **5** cotidianis…sedulis] *transp. TA*

blessed who carries the yoke of the Lord from his childhood, (Jer 2:20) how much more blessed is he who, exceeding the young Benjamin (Gn 49:27) in holiness and purity, having lived the space of around thirty years in the company of the Preachers, and spending the whole of the number of the days of his life in the school of Divine service, even until the triumph of his passion. But the reward of good works is glorious (Wis 3:15); and what labors is one able worthily to retell that the Lord's worker endured, whether in tiresome confessions or in the tumults of preaching?

For so that full days be found in him (Ps 72:10), and that he might II.xii have no unproductive nights, though ordained for man's rest, after a brief sleep he turned toward study and reading and during the time of rest he was occupied with devout prayers and sighs. The day however was devoted to the advantage of souls, whether in daily and painstaking concern for preaching, or in persevering in the hearing of confessions, or rather by inveighing against the pestiferous dogmas of the heretics with powerful arguments, in which he was known to be illuminated by a special gift of grace. Thus the Lord added grace to grace, because in every district the multitudes of the people flocked together to his preaching, and with gratitude he showed the magnitude of his powers. For they burst forth, coming from cities and towns with banners and sounding horns: they followed him in such numbers that only with difficulty was he able to separate himself from them. More often, where he stood up to preach, such an innumerable crowd ran to seize the place beforehand that he was in an intolerable crush. On account of this the people of Milan, as a sign of their devotion, provided a state carriage decorated with painted panels, carried not by the necks of animals, but borne by the shoulders of the faithful, assembled specially for the saint, and saving him inviolate

---

imminendo] immorando *A Taeg*   **6** aut] uel *A*   *add.* contra *P1 P3 Ty Tr*
pestiferum] pestiferam *P1*   **7** confutando] insistendo *P1 Ty Tr* | specialis] speciali
TA   **8** exequauit] adequauit *TA*   **14** intolerabiliter] multipliciter *TA*
15 mediolanensis] Mediolanensium *A* | mediolanensis populus] *transp. N* | in] ob
TA   **16** ex] *add.* peditis *P3 exp.* | animalium] animalia *A*   **17** sanctum] sanum *Ty*
factum *P3 Tr*

multitudinis importune seruabant illesum et predicationis locum
aptius sibi prouidebat ceteris preminentem.

Sic namque deduci dei decebat agricolam: qui semen ueritatis
contra hereses. semen pacis inter odia et aduersus scelera semen
iusticie seminabat. Unde multi abiurabant hereses. catholica
ueritate inspecta. plures dimissis iniuriis finem discordiis
5 imponebant. plurimi sua confitendo peccata ad penitentiam
properabant. Qui enim ministrabat talia semina seminanti. tales
fructus habundantius ex talibus seminibus proferebat. propter
quod labores ei leues et dies pauci. pre diuini amoris magnitudine
uidebantur.

de fiducia eius ad deum

Sicut autem ad labores quoslibet tolerandos amor dei et letitia
reportata de fructuum habundantia. ipsum fortius roborabant. sic
ad aggrediendum queque ardua. superna prouocabat fiducia.
experimentis plurimis comprobata. Sic enim de superno confidebat
5 auxilio: quod credebat. et uere uix esse ita dure ceruicis homines in
ciuitate uel in castro. quin eorum corda salubriter subuerteret: si
tempus adesset predicationi eorum diutius insistendi. Unde si quod
rarissime contigit interdum accideret. quod urbem ingressus uel
oppidum. in prima uel in secunda predicatione copiosum populum
10 non haberet: reuelata predicta fiducia. in solamen sociorum suorum
illud propheticum inducebat. ad huc quadraginta dies et niniue
subuertetur. Quod non solum semel per eum sicut per ionam. nec in

---

II.xiii,6 Qui … 7 habundantius] Mt 3:2   **II.xiv,12** per ionam] Jnh 3

---

18 seruabant] seruabat *TA*   **19** preminentem] prominentem *P1 Ty* preminentiorem
A Taeg no break P1 P2 P3 Ty Tr Ps S F N W Nv   **II.xiii,1** Sic … II.xiii,9 uidebantur]
om. TA add. Unde multi conuenientes ad predicationem eius abiurabant hereses:
catholica ueritate inspecta. Plures dimissis injuriis: finem discordiis imponebant:
plurimi sua confitendo: ad penitentiam properabant *TA* | dei … agricolam] debebat
agricola *Taeg* | decebat] deducebat *exp. du P1* | qui] *om. P1 P3 Tr add.* cum *P3
Tr* | semen] *add.* uero *P1 exp.*   **2** inter] contra *Taeg*   **4** dimissis iniuriis] *transp. Taeg*
5 sua confitendo] *transp. P3*   **8** diuini] *om. Ps W* | diuini amoris] *transp. Taeg*
9 uidebantur] *add.* VIII *P1*   **10** de … deum] *om. P1 P3 Ty Tr TA* | deum] *add.* viii

from the pressured importunings of the multitudes; it provided for him a fit place of preaching more prominent than the others.

This is the treatment that befits a farmer of God, who sows the seed of truth against heresy, the seed of peace in the midst of hatred, and the seed of justice against wickedness. On his account many abjured heresy when confronted by Catholic truth, many forgiving injuries saw the end of discord, many were hurried to penance by the confession of their sins. He sent so many seeds to the Sower, and brought forth such a great crop; on this account how easy the efforts and how few the days seemed to him in light of the magnitude of the love of God (Mt 3:2).   II.xiii

On his trust in God   II.xiv

Moreover, he girded himself for whatever work had to be borne, strengthened by the Love of God and by remembering the joy of an abundant harvest. So he approached whatever difficulties, urged on by heavenly faith, having been tested by many trials. For so much did he trust in heavenly aid that he believed that there scarcely could be men of such stiff necks in either city or countryside that he could not profitably overturn their hearts, if he but had the time to preach to them at length. Therefore when going into a city or village, sometimes his first or second sermon was sparsely attended (though that rarely happened). Showing great trust, he comforted his brethren with the prophecy that there was yet forty days left till the destruction of Nineveh. Unlike Jonah he did not only preach at one time or in one

---

II.xiii,1 This… II.xiv,14 3] Taegio, 1.10.

---

capitulum *N* viii. *W*   **II.xiv,1** Sicut… II.xiv,4 comprobata] *om. TA* | letitia] letitiam *P3* | letitia… 2 reportata] *transp. Taeg*   **4** plurimis] pluribus *Taeg* comprobata] approbata *Tr* | enim] *add.* ipse *T* | confidebat… 5 auxilio] *om. Ps* **5** credebat] *add.* sic erat *TA* | et uere] *om. P1 P3 Tr Ty* | esse] esset *TA*   **6** uel] *add.* in *P1 P3 Tr Ty* | corda salubriter] *transp. P2 F S Ps W*   **9** in²] *om. TA*   **10** sociorum] sanctorum *P3*   **11** inducebat] *add.* aa *P3 exp. add. al. man. sin.* non | quadraginta] LX *Nv*   **12** solum] *om. N TA add. sup. F* | per¹… ionam] semel per se uel per eum sicut ionam *P1 om. TA*

una ciuitate tantum. sed multociens et in multis constat esse completum.

de miraculis eius in uita et primo de loquela muti.

Cum autem sicut pluuia doctrina eius concresceret: inter ipsos eloquiorum imbres quasi effusos celitus. domino cooperante et sermonem confirmante sequentibus signis. plura ceperunt miracula coruscare. Dum enim die quadam mediolani pre foribus ecclesie beati
5   eustorgii predicaret. cuidam iuueni muto ad eum ex populi deuotione adducto. immisso digito in os eius. ad conficiendum sacrosanctum corpus christi hactenus consecrato: soluto uinculo lingue eius beneficium loquele restituit. mox enim interrogatus puer qui siluerat decem annis. quid habuisset in ore. digitum inquit uestrum. Et statim
10 coram omnibus in uberes gratiarum actiones erumpens. apertorum nouiter christo reddidit uitulos labiorum: propter quod iniqua loquentium hereticorum labia. pre confusione obstrui debuissent. sed ipsi tanquam canes impudentissimi salutifera confusione non sunt confusi: et erubescere nescierunt: unde ad sancti sui gloriam plura
15 signa innouauit dominus: et mirabilia inmutauit.

II.xv,1 ipsos … 2 celitus] Dt 32:2   **11** nouiter … labiorum] Mk 7:31

---

13 multis] *add.* locis *TA Taeg*   **14** completum] *add.* xi. *P1*   **15** de¹] Exemplum de *N* | de¹ … muti] *om. P1 P3 Ty Tr TA* | in uita] *om. N* | muti] *add.* ix capitulum *N* ix. *W* **II.xv,2** celitus] *add.* et *P1*   **3** plura] multa *P1 P3 Ty Tr*   **4** coruscare] *add.* in uita quoque ipsius sanctitas eius latere non potuit: qui miraculorum claritate pateret. *TA* | die quadam] *transp. P1 P3 Ty Tr*   **5** iuueni muto] *transp. P1 P3 Ty Tr* | populi deuotione] *transp. Taeg*   **6** os] ore *Taeg* | conficiendum … 7 consecrato] corpus christi conficiendum *Taeg* | sacrosanctum … 7 christi] corpus christi sacrosanctum *P1*   **8** beneficium loquele] *transp. Taeg* | enim] *om. Taeg* | siluerat … 9 decem] diu tacuerat, id est decem *Taeg*   **9** habuisset … ore] in ore habuisset *Taeg*   **10** coram] *add.* hominibus *P1 P3 Ty Tr* | coram … erumpens] omnibus in gratiarum actiones erumpens *TA* in uberes gratiarum actiones coram omnibus erumpens *Taeg* apertorum] actorum *P3*   **11** reddidit] reddit *P1 P3 Ty* | reddidit … labiorum] uitulos labiorum reddidit *Taeg*   **12** loquentium] *om. N* | loquentium hereticorum] *transp. P1 P3 Ty Tr* | hereticorum] *om. Taeg* | obstrui] *add.* debent *P3 exp.*   **13** tanquam]

place, but filled many times and places with his agreeable teaching (Jnh 3).

On the miracles that he performed while living, and firstly of healing a mute boy

His teaching dropped like rain among the showers of his eloquence, as if it were dropped from heaven (Dt 32:2). By the help of the Lord his sermons were confirmed by mighty signs, and many miracles began to occur. One day, when he was preaching in Milan in front of the entrance to the church of Sant'Eustorgio, a mute youth was led to him by the piety of the crowd. He placed his finger – which had been consecrated to confect the Body of Christ – in the boy's mouth. At this, the chain on his tongue was relased and good of speech was restored. He asked the boy who had been mute for so long (nearly ten years) what he had in his mouth. "Your finger," he said and at once erupted in abundant thanksgiving in the sight of all, and returned an offering to Christ from his newly opened lips (Mk 7:31); on account of this the iniquitous lips of the heretics ought to be stopped up with shame, yet those most brazen dogs are not upset by salutary confutation and are ignorant of shame, though for the glory of His saint the Lord revealed many wonders and worked many miracles.

II.xv,1 His…II.xv,16 miracles] Taegio, 2.11.

---

tamquam *Taeg* **14** unde] *add.* adhuc *P1 P3 Tr* | ad] *om. S* | gloriam] *add.* adhuc *Ty* **15** signa…dominus] innouauit signa *Taeg* | inmutauit] *om. Taeg* add x *P1*

de nube extorta in refrigerium estus

Nam quadam die cum apud mediolanum quedam episcopum
catharorum beatus petrus examinaret. multis episcopis et religiosis et
maxima copia ciuitatis ad hoc spectaculum congregatis. et dies tum ex
predicatione tum ex hereticorum examinatione in longum protracta
5   fuisset. et maximus estus cunctos affligeret. heresiarcha ille. tempore
subsannationis inuento. cepit coram omnibus exclamare. O Petre
peruerse si tu es ita sanctus sicut hic stultus populus te affirmat. cur
ipsum permittis tam grauiter estuare. et non rogas dominum ut
nubem aliquam interponat. ut non moriatur hic stultus populus tanto
10   estu? Cui cum athleta fidei fiducialiter respondisset. quod dixerat se
facturum: si promitteret quod heresi protinus abiurata. conuerteretur
ad fidem. multi ex catholicis super obligatione beati petri contristari
ceperunt. timentes ne fides catholica ex hoc confusioni pateret. et
econuerso multi ex infidelibus sunt gauisi. confusionem uiri sancti
15   cum desiderio prestolantes. precipue cum in toto aere nulla uel
minima nubecula appareret penitus. proinde ut secure promitteret
suum episcopum cum clamoribus infestabant. Cumque isto modo
pertinatia heretici se obligare nolentis frangi non posset uel
aliquatenus emolliri. beatus petrus qui propter infidelium gaudium
20   uel timorem fidelium. sperans in domino non fuerat infirmatus. ut
appareat inquit quod bonus deus omnium uisibilium et inuisibilium

---

16 de…estus] *om. P1 P3 Ty Tr TA* | estus] *add.* x capitulum *N* x. *W*
II.xvi,1 Nam] *om. TA* | quadam] quodam *P1 Ty Tr* quodem *P3* | cum] *om. TA*
2 catharorum] hereticorum *TA* | beatus petrus] beatum petrum *A* | episcopis…
religiosis] religiosis episcopis *TA*   **3** tum…4 examinatione] quia *TA*   **4** protracta]
prostracta *T*   **5** heresiarcha] *add.* illa. *Ps exp.*   **6** subsannationis] subsannacionis *T*
7 stultus populus] *transp. P1 P3 Ty Tr N*   **8** dominum] deum tuum *TA*   **9** ut…
populus] ne moriatur *TA*   **11** heresi…abiurata] quod abiurata heresi *TA*   **13** ne]
add. ex *P3 exp.* | hoc] *add.* uisio *P3 exp.* | confusioni pateret] confusionem
pateretur *Taeg*   **14** econuerso] conuerso *A* | ex] *om. P3 add. al. marg. sin.* | sancti]
om. A Taeg   **15** precipue] *om. P1 P3 Ty Tr* | in] *sup. P1*   **16** appareret penitus]
transp. P2 S F Ps N W TA   **17** suum…cum] *om. TA* | clamoribus] clamore *P1 P2
P3 Ty Tr* | Cumque] *add.* uel *S*   **18** pertinatia heretici] *transp. Taeg* | uel…19
emolliri] *om. TA*   **19** aliquatenus] *add.* ememoliri *P3 exp.* | qui…20 fidelium] *om.*

Of the cloud he obtained for relief from the heat II.xvi

One day Blessed Peter was examining a Cathar bishop at Milan, a great multitude of bishops and religious along with a greater part of the city had come together to witness the event, but the day grew long, whether from preaching or from examination of the heretic, and a great heat began to afflict all those assembled. The heresiarch resorted to derision, and he began to exclaim in the presence of all, "O perverse Peter, if you are as holy as this stupid mob here thinks you are, why do you permit them to be so greatly afflicted by heat, and why don't you ask God to make a cloud to cover them, so that these foolish people might not die from heat?" The athlete of the faith trustingly responded that he would do so if the heretic would promise that he would immediately abjure his heresy and be converted to the faith. Many of the Catholics began to be worried about the obligation undertaken by Blessed Peter, fearing that the Catholic faith might suffer embarrassment. On the other hand, many of the unfaithful heretics were full of joy, awaiting his confutation with gladness, especially since there was not the least trace of a cloud in the sky. They began to harass their bishop with shouts so that he would promise. And in this way the obstinate heretics forced him to swear. Though the bishop had been unwilling to obligate himself, he was unable to discourage or in any way soften them. Blessed Peter, not weakened by the joy of the infidels nor the fear of the faithful, trusting in the Lord that He might make a cloud appear, said, "Because the Good God was creator and fashioner of all things visible

---

17 Of…II.xvi,11 do] Innocent IV, "Magnis et crebris" Canonization Bull; LA 422-423; Taegio, 1.5. **II.xvi,1** Blessed…Milan] LA 423-424; VF, 238; Taegio, 4.31. The Vitas Fratrum adds "who had been captured at that time." This is perhaps the dispute with Albert of Bergamo which is referred to in the *Summa against the Heretics* of disputed authorship. See: Petrus Martyr (Attr.), *Summa contra Hereticos ad Petrum Martyrem Attributa*, Medium Aevum Monographs 38 (n.s.) (Oxford: The Society for the Study of Modern Languages and Literature, 2020)

TA | gaudium…20 fidelium] *om. S* **20** fidelium] *add.* gaudium u *W exp.* non…infirmatus] *om. Taeg* **21** inquit] *om. TA*

sit creator et factor: rogo ipsum ut ad consolationem in se credentium. et non credentium confutationem. aliquam dignetur nobis nubeculam mittere. que inter solem et populum interposita nos

25 defendere ualeat ab hoc estu. Quod ubi de quodam pulpito eminenti permisso signaculo crucis expleuit. mox dominus de quadam nube quasi tentorium eis fecit que umbre sue per longum tempus omni populo prebuit uelamentum: et causam exultandi adauxit fidelibus et contra hereticos insultandi.

de mirabili obmutescentia garrulantium hereticorum

Altera etiam die similiter ad disputandum cum hereticis constituta. morantibus fratribus de uicinis conuentibus aduocatis. filii tenebrarum prudentiores filiis lucis. cum essent armis ueritatis exuti: se multitudine armauerunt. ut quem ratione non poterant saltem

5 multiloquio superarent. Affuit insuper eorum stipatus frequentia quidam quem elegerant sue perfidie defensorem. uir clamosus et garrulus et maliciosus. sermonum uersutiis eruditus. Is ubi pugilem fidei cum socio suo conspexisset adstantem. statim uerborum laqueos eius pedibus preparauit: et ut incautum corruere faceret. cepit

10 importune ac clamose insistere. ut ad ea que proposuerat responderet. Quo sepius conclamante. uir dei attendens quod seruum dei contentiosis clamoribus litigare non decet. et ubi non erat auditus. uerba ueritatis et sobrietatis effundere non prodesset. recordatus

---

II.xvii,2 filii … 3 lucis] Lk 16:8   **11** uir … 13 prodesset] 2 Tm 2:14-16

---

22 et factor] *om. TA*   **23** confutationem] confusionem *A Taeg* | dignetur … 24 nobis] *transp. P1 P3 P5 Ty Tr*   **24** interposita] posita *TA*   **25** quodam] *add.* et *P1 exp.* | pulpito] populus *Ty exp. add. al. man. dex.* pulpito   **26** de … nube] *om. Tr om. P1 add. marg. dex.* nu *om. P3 add. al. marg. sin.* de quadam nubecula *om. Ty add.* nubem   **27** eis fecit] *transp. P3*   **30** de … hereticorum] *om. P1 P3 Ty Tr TA* garrulantium hereticorum] xi capitulum *N* xi. *W*   **II.xvii,2** morantibus … aduocatis] *om. TA*   **3** prudentiores … lucis] *om. TA* | armis ueritatis] *transp. TA*   **4** saltem] *om. TA*   **6** quem] quoniam *P3* | clamosus … 7 maliciosus] linguosus clamosus et maliciosus *P1 P3 Tr Ty*   **7** uersutiis] uersuciis *T* | Is] hiis *T* his *A*   **9** eius pedibus] *om. T* | et … faceret] *om. TA* | cepit] cepitque *TA add.* et ut

and invisible, I ask Him that, as a consolation to the faithful who believe in Him and as an embarrassment to the non-believers, He might deign to send to us some small cloud, which shall interpose itself between the sun and the people, and might serve to defend us from this heat." From his high pulpit he finished, having made the sign of the cross. Suddenly the Lord set a cloud over them as if like a tent, which served for a long period as His shadow over all the people, and was a cause for exultation among the faithful and a mock against the heretics.

Of the wondrous silencing of a chattering heretic   II.xvii

Another day found him similarly disputing with heretics. Peter called for aid from brethren tarrying in nearby convents. The sons of darkness are shrewder than the sons of light (Lk 16:8) since they have removed the armor of truth and have armed themselves with many other things. They were not able to use reason but rather sought to win by loquaciousness. A crowd of heretics came, and from among them they elected one to see to their perfidious defense, a noisy man given to barking and babbling, a man of wicked words and cunning erudition. He had observed the champion of the faith standing with his companions and immediately prepared a snare of words for his feet. So that he might serve to overthrow the unexpecting man, he began to importune him rudely in a loud voice, trying to provoke Peter into responding. To this repeated abuse the man of God observed that it did not befit a servant of God to dispute by shouting. And where he was not heard, the words of truth and sobriety would benefit no one. (2 Tm 2: 14-16) Having recalled the mercy of the

---

II.xvii,1 Another...II.xvii,1 heretics] VF, 238; Taegio, 4.32

---

incautum corruere faceret et importune *Ps exp.*   **10** importune ac] *om. Tr add. al. man. dex.* | ac] *et A* | proposuerat] *posuerat P3* **11** conclamante] *exclamante Ps acclamante P2 Taeg* **12** clamoribus] *sermonibus TA* | erat] *est Ps* **13** recordatus... 14 domini] *om. TA*

misericordi tue domini totum se ad orationem contulit. deuote
15 supplicans ut hostes uel iuste erubescerent tanquam impii. et muta
fierent labia dolosa: aut misericorditer super eos sol uere intelligentie
oriretur. Nec mora. mox duorum alterum quod petiit impetrauit:
prout utriusque partis merita exigebant. Cum enim defensor fidei
fiducialiter insisteret aduersus ueritatis aduersarium. ut adhuc quereret
20 quod querebat. ita diuine uirtuti dyabolica uerba cesserunt. ut ille
paulo ante loquax et garrulus. sic subito mutus. quasi. factus est et
elinguis. ut nec ad querendum nec ad respondendum aperire os ad
uerbum unicum preualeret; propter quod eiusdem perfidie comites
infideles dissipati sunt ab inuicem: nec compuncti. eorumdem
25 duritia resistente.

de curatione tumoris gule ad tactum cappe

Semel autem contigit eo iter agente cum episcopo placentino. quod
ad domum diuerterent uiri nobilis domini Gaufridi comitis de
lomello cuius filium henricum nomine ita tumor gule compresserat.
quod nec loqui poterat nec spirare: propter quod parentes eius de
5 proxima filii morte anxii et desperati de uita. audito fratris petri
ueronensis aduentu. ambo properant in aduenientis occursum. et
moriturum puerum dolenter nunciant et sollicite recommendant.
Quo accedente leuatis ad deum manibus. et crucis in eo facto
signaculo. puer iam deuotus suo languenti collo. tamquam aliquod
10 salutare remedium capam eius adhibuit: et benedictione recepta
recepit insimul sanitatem. Quod pater diligenter atque libenter

---

14 tue] *om. P3 N Taeg* | totum] totumque *A* | deuote] *om. TA*   **15** erubescerent]
add. te *P3 exp.*   **16** aut] uel *TA* | uere intelligentie] *om. Ps*   **17** quod] *add.* petrus
P3 Tr   **18** partis] *om. P1 P3 Ty Tr*   **19** adhuc] *add.* proponeret et *TA*   **20** ita...
cesserunt] *om. TA* | ut] *sup. P1*   **25** resistente] *add.* xii *P1*   **26** de...cappe] *om. P1*
P3 Ty Tr TA | cappe] *add.* xii capitulum *N* xii. uuuuuuu *W line filler*
II.xviii,2 uiri...domini] *om. Ps W* | Gaufridi] Gaufredi *Ps W A Taeg*   **3** lomello]
lumello *N* | compresserat] oppresserat *P1 P3 Ty Tr*   **6** properant] preperant *P1 Ty*
8 deum] celum *A Taeg Ps*   **9** suo] sub *P1 P3 Ty Tr add.* tam *TA Taeg*

Lord, he completely composed himself in devoted prayer, begging that his enemies might rightly blush for shame just as the impious do, and that their cunning lips would fall mute, or that the true sun of wisdom should mercifully appear to him. Without delay, the former of the two requests was suddenly granted as he had asked. For when the defender of the faith trustingly set forth in opposition to the enemies of truth, that which he strove for he obtained, for Divine power silenced the devilish talk, so that he who a little while before was wordy and babbling, was suddenly made mute and speechless, so that neither in asking nor in responding did his mouth have any power to utter a single word. On account of this the treacherous accomplices of his perfidy were confounded among themselves, but were not brought to repentance, since they continued in their hardness of spirit.

On the cure of a throat tumor by the touch of Peter's cappa.   II.xviii

Once it happened that, while making a journey with the Bishop of Piacenza, they diverted to the house of the nobleman Gaufredus, Count of Lomello, whose son Henry suffered from a throat tumor. He was neither able to speak or to breathe. On account of this his parents were concerned that their son might be near death, and despaired of his life. Having heard of the arrival of Peter of Verona, both hastened to meet him and relate sorrowfully that their son was about to die, entrusting the matter to him with anxiety. Having arrived, he lifted his hands to heaven and made the sign of the cross. The devout boy placed his cappa as a salutary remedy on his sick neck. Having received the blessing, he was restored to health. His father carefully watched this with joy and bought a new cappa for

---

II.xviii,1 Once...II.xviii,14 foolishness] LA, 424; Bull of Canonization; Taegio, 4.33. | Bishop...2 Piacenza] Bishop Albert, Piacenza 1244–1261, Ferrara 1261–1274.

aspiciens: empta illi noua capa tante uirtutis uestimentum uetus sibi retinuit quod postmodum nequaquam ad insipientiam ei cessit.

de proiectione uermis uillosi ad tactam eiusdem cappe

Procedente siquidem tempore idem nobilis uehementi uiscerum torsione grauatus. credens et metuens exinde sibi mortis imminere discrimen. capam ipsam quam ex tunc conseruauerat reuerenter fecit afferri. qua suo apposita pectori. mox uermem quendam duo 5 habentem capita et pilorum densitate uillosum euomuit. plene statim sanitatis consecutus effectum.

de curatione cuiusdam contracte

Dum uero in conspectu magnatum magnificaret dominus sanctum suum: non minus pauperibus et religiosis erat affabilis aut amabilis habebatur speciali deuotionis affectu. Quibus cum frequenter gratiam uisitationis impenderet. flammas inter eos diuini amoris accendens. 5 confirmans uacillantes sermonibus suis. confortans manus remissas et genua trementia roborans. contigit ut in quodam burgo mediolanensis dyocesis nomine caracte ad humiliatorum domum prout consueuerat declinaret; ubi ad quamdam de sororibus nomine carasiam. que corporis uiribus sic totaliter destituta iacebat et iacuerat 10 annis septem. quod pro qualicumque necessitate non ualuerat surgere nec ualebat. a quibusdam de ipsius suffragio confidentibus est perductus; ad quam perueniens sic orauit. domine qui sanasti paraliticum et lazarum suscitasti: obsecro ut huic digneris etiam

---

12 uirtutis] *add.* efficatiam admirans *TA Taeg* | sibi] quod *P1 om. F Ps P3 Ty Tr W N* 13 quod] *om. P1* | postmodum] *add.* ad insip *P3 exp.* | ei cessit] *transp. N* cessit] *add.* xiii *P1* 14 de...cappe] *om. P1 P3 Ty Tr TA* | uillosi] pilosi *Ps* | cappe] *add.* 13 capitulum *N* xiii *W* **II.xix,2** exinde sibi] *om. P1 P3 Ty Tr* 3 discrimen] discrimine *A add.* exinde sibi *P1 P3 Ty Tr* | ex] et *Ps* 4 duo...5 habentem] *transp. TA* 5 plene] plena *TA* | statim] *om. TA* 6 sanitatis...effectum] liberatione et sanitate secura *TA* | effectum] *add.* xiiii *P1* 7 de...contracte] *om. P1 P3 Ty Tr TA* | contracte] *add.* xiiii capitulum *N* xiiii. *W* **II.xx,1** Dum] Cum *P1 Ty Tr F.* *This may be an issue of initals filled in later in the sub-archetype; e.g. P3 has no initals.* Dum...II.xx,6 roborans] *om. TA* | uero] *add.* sic *P2 S F Ps W N* 2 et] *om. P1 P3 Ty Tr* 3 speciali] specialis *P1 P3 Ty Tr N Taeg* | gratiam...4 uisitationis] *transp.*

Peter. He considered that the old vestment retained great power. Peter could not dissuade him from his foolishness.

On the expelling of a hairy worm by the touch of the same cappa. II.xix

Some time later the same nobleman, suffering a grave pain in the bowels, believing and fearing himself to be in the imminent danger of death, reverently took up the cappa that he had carefully preserved till then, and held it to his chest. Suddenly he vomited forth a worm with two heads and shaggy, dense hair, and immediately he was made healthy.

On the cure of one whose movements were restricted II.xx

Truly the Lord magnified his saint in the presence of great men, but he was not any less accessible and lovable towards the poor and religious, and he had special devotion and affection for them. He granted them the grace of frequent visits and, with the fire of divine charity burning between them, he confirmed the weak with his words, he comforted drooping hands and reinforced trembling knees. Once he was in a town of the Diocese of Milan called Carate. He diverted to the house of the Humiliati, as he was accustomed to. He visited a sister there named Carasia, whose strength of body had abandoned her and who had lain immobile for seven years. She was unable to arise for any necessity nor could she get any stronger. She was brought to him by those confident in his ability to assist. And coming to her he prayed thus, "O Lord, who healed the paralytic and raised Lazarus, I beseech that You would deign to grant health to this woman." She

---

II.xx,1 Truly … II.xx,18 faculties] Taegio, 4.34.

Taeg **4** inter … amoris] diuini amoris inter eos *P1 P3 Ty* inter eos *Tr add. al man.* dex. **7** caracte] carate *P2 S F Ps W Nv* carathe *N add.* ut *P1* **9** carasiam] carasina *Ps* | sic] *om. P3 add. al. man.* dex. | totaliter] *om. A Taeg* **10** non] nec *A Taeg* **12** perueniens] ueniens *A Taeg* | orauit] adorauit *P1* | qui] *add.* me *Tr exp.* sanasti … **13** paraliticum] *transp. Taeg* **13** ut … digneris] quod digneris huic *P2 S F Ps N W* ut digneris huic *A Taeg*

mulieri concedere sanitatem. Que protinus liberata eodem sero de suo
grabato consurgens sequenti mane. redeunti occurrit; quamdiu uixit.
sex annis uidelicet perseuerans incolumis. et ad officia pristina plenius
restituta.

de curatione alterius

Simile autem apud mediolanum contigisse probatur. ubi cum quidam
nomine acerbus per quinque annos sic mansisset contractus. ut per
terram in sextario traheretur: ad beatum petrum adductus. ab eo
signatus continuo sanatus surrexit.

de corporali et spirituali curatione mulieris desparate de uita

Meritus etiam serui dei ueniam de peccatis mereri potuit similiter et
sperare quedam mulier mantuana. de qua plurimi desperabant. In
mortis enim discrimine constituta: per longum temporis spatium iam
perdiderat usum lingue; ad quam rogatus accedens. ut ad eam uita
ualeret ingredi per auditum et mors egredi per loquelam. caputio
reuerenter extracto. premisso dominus uobiscum. primam lectionem
sancti euangelii secundum ioannem. primitus eam audire fecit: et
mox ut confitendo peccata sibi loqueretur iniunxit; qua incipiente uti
obedientia. uel gratia potius salutari. stupefacti circumstantes ac leti.
de domo egressi sunt. ne peccata confitentis audirent. sed postmodum
sic fortiter loqui cepit. quod generalem confessionem quam fecit. in
fine. distincte audire et intelligere potuerant extra domum; propter
quod fama ipsius et gratia non solum in ciuitate predicta. sed ubique

---

14 concedere sanitatem] *transp. A Taeg* | suo] *om. A Taeg* **15** sequenti] *om. A Taeg* | uixit] iussit *S exp.* uixit *add. al. man. sin.* uiuit *Ps* **16** sex] se *T* | annis uidelicet] *transp. A Taeg* | officia pristina] *transp. A Taeg* | plenius] plene *Taeg om. TA add.* ro *P3 exp.* **17** restituta] *add.* xv *P1* **18** de…alterius] *om. P1 P3 Ty Tr TA* | alterius] *add.* xv capitulum *N* xv. *W* **II.xxi,1** autem] accidisse *Taeg* contigisse] *om. Taeg* **2** acerbus] aserbus *F S Ps N W* | mansisset] permansisset *Ps* mansit *Taeg* **3** adductus] aduectus *P1* **4** surrexit] *add.* xvi *P1* **5** de[1]…uita] *om. P1 P3 Ty Tr TA* | uita] *add.* 16 capitulum *N* xvi. *W* **II.xxii,1** dei] *add.* tur *P1 exp.* **4** usum lingue] *transp. A Taeg* **5** mors] in ore *P1 P3 Ty Tr* more *W* **6** premisso… uobiscum] dominus uobiscum premisso *P1 P3 Ty Tr* | primam lectionem] prima lectionem *F* prima lectione *T* **7** secundum] *add.* iho *P3 exp.* | eam] *om. P3 add. al.*

was immediately freed that very evening and, rising from her cot the following morning, she ran to meet him whenever he returned as long as she lived, namely six more years, remaining unimpaired and fully restored to her former faculties.

The cure of another one

A similar event was known to have occurred near Milan, where a boy named Asserbus had endured a similar weakness for five years, so much that he had to be dragged about in a bushel basket. He was led to Saint Peter and, at his sign, arose immediately healed.

Of the bodily and spiritual cure of a woman who despaired of life.

A woman of Mantua was able to hope for and to earn remission of her sins, which oppressed her by their great number, by the merits of the servant of God. Confronted with the crisis of death, she had for a long period of time lost use of her voice. She begged Peter to come to her asked whether she might be able to enter life through hearing, and escape death through his speech. Peter, having reverently removed his hood, said "The Lord be with you," and she began to hear for the first time the beginning of the Gospel according to John. Next, so that by speaking she might confess her sin, he enjoined her: "anything received ought to be used in obedience or with grace preferably for the purpose of salvation." The bystanders, astonished and happy, left the house, so that they would not hear her confessing her sins. Later she began to speak loudly, and made a general confession, which she completed, and it was able to be heard and understood outside the house. On account of this Peter's fame and reputation were spread

---

II.xxi,1 A…II.xxi,4 healed] LA, 424; Taegio 4.34.   **II.xxii,1** A…II.xxii,21 witnesses] Taegio, 2.12.

---

man. dex.   **8** ut] *add.* contend *exp. Ps add.* al man. *sup. P3* | confitendo] confiteretur *A Taeg* **9** uel] f *P3* | gratia potius] *transp. P3 Ty* | salutari] *add.* et *P1 exp.*   **10** sed postmodum] sic que postmodum *T* siquidem postmodum *A* sed postea sic *Taeg* **11** generalem] *add.* conff *P3 exp.*   **12** potuerant] potuerunt *A Taeg* **13** ubique] usque *P3 fort.* sicque

per patriam cotidie augebatur. et diffusius rutilabat. nec mirum quia
15 hec et alia plura dum uiueret dignatus est per eum dominus operari;
plures enim energuminos et alios uariis uexatos languoribus solo tactu
uel crucis signaculo liberauit. sicut plurium fide dignorum
attestationibus est probatum.

III Uerum cum pestis heretica in lombardie prouincia pullularet. et
multas iam ciuitates contagione pestifera infecisset; summus pontifex
dominus innocentius. quartus attendens quantum foret ouibus
luporum perniciosa commixtio: ad pestem diabolicam abolendam.
5 diuersos inquisitores de ordine predicatorum. quasi diuersos canes qui
lupos arcere ualerent a gregibus. in diuersis lombardie partibus
prouidentius delegauit. sed cum apud mediolanum heretici non
solum multi numero sed etiam magni seculari potentia. acuti
fraudulentia. eloquentia garruli et diabolica pleni sciencia resident:
10 summus pontifex sciens et intelligens beatum petrum uirum esse
magnanimem. qui ab hostium multitudine non paueret:
animaduertens quoque sue uirtutis constantiam. per quam et
aduersariorum potencie nec in modico cederet. cognoscens etiam eius
facundiam per quam fallacias hereticorum detegeret: non ignorans
15 insuper ipsum in diuina plene sapientia eruditum. per quam friuola
hereticorum argumenta rationabiliter confutaret. utpote inter

---

14 cotidie] *om. Taeg* | cotidie augebatur] *transp. P1 P3 Ty Tr* | quia] *om. TA*
quia…18 probatum] *om. TA* **15** et] *add.* alia *TA Taeg* | alia] *om. P1 P3 Ty Tr*
plura] *add.* signa et miracula *TA* | uiueret] uideret *Ps* | per…operari] dominus per
eum operari *Tr* | operari] *add.* et *P3* **16** energuminos] energumenos *A Taeg* | alios
uariis] aliis *T* | languoribus] languoribus u *sup. P1* langoribus *S F Ps W T*
17 crucis signaculo] signo crucis *Taeg* crucis signa *A* | plurium] plurimorum *A Taeg*
18 probatum] *add.* de executione inquisitionis inuiute <inuente? iniuncte? *dub.*>
contra hereticos per apostolicam sedem *P2 Ps F N add.* 17 capitulum *N* xvii. *W*
III.i,1 heretica] hereticam *A* **3** dominus] *om. P1 P3 Ty Tr TA Taeg* | quartus] iiii
P1 Tr | attendens…4 commixtio] *om. TA Taeg and from Legenda Aurea as well.*
foret] fieret *Taeg* **4** perniciosa] peruiciosa *P2 Tr N* **6** arcere] arcerent *T* arcerent
corr. arcere *Tr* | ualerent] possent *TA Taeg* **7** prouidentius] *om. T* | apud] *om. A
Taeg* | mediolanum] mediolani*A Taeg* **8** magni] *add.* in *P1 P3 Ty Tr* | acuti…9
fraudulentia] *om. Ps* **9** eloquentia] *add.* et *TA* | garruli] garrulosi *A Taeg*

not only in Mantua but were everywhere magnified and diffused daily throughout the countryside. The Lord deigned to work not only these but many other wonders through him when he lived, for many possessed persons and those having various other complaints were healed solely by his touch or by the sign of the cross, as is proven by the testimony of many worthy witnesses.

When the heretical plague was sprouting in Lombardy and many   III.i
cities were already infected by their pestilential influence, the Sovereign Pontiff Lord Innocent IV alluded to the great danger of lambs mixed with wolves. For the destruction of the devilish plague, he providentially deputed various inquisitors of the Order of Preachers (as dogs who are able to keep the wolves from the flock) into the various parts of Lombardy. But as for the heretics of Milan, where not only were they large in number, but also possessed of great worldly power, severe in wickedness, chattering in speech and full of devilish knowledge, the pope, knowing Blessed Peter to be a man of magnanimity, sent him as one who would not be frightened by a multitude of enemies. He knew the steadfastness of his virtue, by which constancy he would not yield to the power of adversaries in any way. He was also aware of his eloquence, by which he would break to pieces the fallacies of the heretics, nor did he forget that Peter was also abundantly learned in divine wisdom, with which he would be able rationally to refute all of the frivolous arguments of the heretics. He remembered how he was turned away from heretics as a

---

III.i,1 When...25 him] LA, 424-425; Taegio, 4.30. **6** dogs] Pun on 'Dominicans', *Domini Canes*, the hounds of the Lord.

---

diabolica...sciencia] *om. TA* | sciencia] *add.* Idem *TA Taeg* **10** et intelligens] *om.* *TA* | uirum...11 magnanimem] esse magnanimem uirum *P1 P3 Ty Tr TA* **11** hostium] ostium *S* **12** animaduertens] aduertens *A Taeg* | et] *om. TA* **13** cognoscens] recognoscens *TA add.* et *P3 exp.* **14** non...16 confutaret] *om. S add. al. man. sin.* **15** ipsum] eum *P1 P3 Ty Tr T* | in diuina] mundana *A Taeg* plene] *om. Tr add. al. man. sin.* **16** rationabiliter] *om. TA* | utpote...19 edoctus] *om. TA LA*

hereticos a puero conuersatus. et qualiter sensum peruerterent scripturarum. et quibus uerbis suam cauteriatam conscientiam palliarent. frequentibus pugnis et diuinis experimentis edoctus. ipsum tam strenuum fidei pugilem. et tam indefessum domini bellatorem. in mediolano et in eius comitatu instituit. et inquisitorem heretice prauitatis. auctoritate concessa plenaria ordinauit.

Ipse igitur iniunctum sibi officium diligenter exercens sampsonis uulpeculas perquirebat et dissipabat ubique: nullam eis requiem tribuens. sed mirabiliter omnes confundens. potenter expellens ita ut non possent resistere sapienti et spiritui qui loquebatur per eum. ad hec inerat beato pugili specialis certandi fiducia contra hostes. ex diuina reuelatione infusa. Nam dum semel aliquantulum ex futuris et incertis euentibus pauidus. ante altare uirginis agones suos uirgini commendaret. per uirginem dormitanti uirgini est responsum. quod per filium uirginis imminente passionis agone. dudum fuit alteri petro dictum. ego rogaui pro te petre ut non deficiat fides tua. Unde nec eum fiducia certa diffisum. nec feruor indefessus tepidum: nec experientia timidum permittebant. Sed sicut leo fortissimus bestiarum ad nullius pauens occursum. pluries hostibus offerebat: sub tali conditione congressum. quod ipsi uidelicet secum ducerent omnes quos possent de toto exercitu scripturarum. Ipse uero contentus esset uno milite contra eos. beatum paulum exprimens et eligens. uelut inuictum pugilem. contra omnes fidei peruersores. Frequenter etiam

---

III.ii,1 sampsonis...2 uulpeculas] Jdg 15:1–7   10 ego...tua] Lk 22:32

---

17 et] *ut P1 P3 Tr* | peruerterent] *om. P3*   **18** cauteriatam] sauciatam *Taeg*
19 frequentibus] *add.* diuinis *P3 exp.*   **20** et...bellatorem] *om. TA* | domini]
pugilem *P3 exp.*   **22** ordinauit] *no break P1 P2 P3 Ty Tr Ps S F N W Nv*
III.ii,1 igitur] *add.* beatus petrus *TA* | sibi officium] beneficium sibi *P3*
sampsonis] sansonis *S F Ps W*   **2** eis] sibi *P1 P3 Ty Tr TA*   **3** confundens] *add.* et
P1 | potenter expellens] *om. TA*   **4** eum] *add.* break *Nv*   **5** hec] hoc *Tr add.* enim
P1   **6** diuina] *add.* sibi *T*   **7** altare] *add.* beate *TA Taeg*   **8** commendaret] *add.* et
Ps | responsum] responssi *P1*   **12** experientia] experiencia *T add.* tepidum *P3 exp.*
14 secum...omnes] omnes secum ducerent *P1 P3 Ty Tr TA*   **16** exprimens]
experimens *A Taeg*   **17** etiam] et *P3*

boy and how they perverted the sense of the scriptures, though by these interpretations they shrewdly salve their condemned consciences. Having been trained by many fights and divine experiences to be a vigorous champion for the faith and an indefatigable battler for the Lord, the pope created Peter inquisitor of heretical depravity for Milan and its environs, and conferred the plenitude of authority upon him.

Therefore, diligently exercising the office conferred on him, he searched everywhere for the foxes of Samson (Jdg 15:1–7) and dispersed them wherever they were, giving them no rest at all, but wonderfully confounding them and powerfully expelling them all, they were not able to withstand his wisdom and the Spirit which spoke through him. In addition to these, a special certitude of faith against his enemies was granted to the blessed fighter, by the pouring forth of divine revelation. For instance, once somewhat uncertain about the future and fearful about some events, he commended his troubles to the Virgin before the Mary Altar. The Virgin responded to the sleeping virgin, "Just as it was said to the other Peter by the Son of the Virgin when the time of His passion was imminent: 'I have prayed for you Peter, that your faith may not fail.'" (Lk 22:32) Thenceforth he never despaired of his certain faith nor was his unwearied fervor made tepid, nor did his experiences permit him to be timid, but as the lion is the strongest of the animals, (Pr 30:30) frightened to meet nothing, frequently he offered debates to enemies under the condition that they would able to cite all of the books of the Bible while he was content fighting against them with just one, choosing a letter of Blessed Paul's. He was the unconquered champion of the faith against all who would pervert it. He also

III.ii

III.ii,1 Therefore…III.iv,24 brethren] Taegio, 4.30; LA 425.   **6** In…13 2232] VF, 239.

hereticis se in ignem proiicere obtulit pro ueritate fidei astruenda si eius in igne comites fieri consentirent.

Insuper pro fide uitam suam non solum periculis. sed morti exponere auidus. forsitan ex diuina reuelatione accepit. quod tam fideliter et frequenter prophetico spiritu proferebat in medium. Nam quasi de suo felici martyrio et etiam de loco proprie sepulture securus.
5 utrumque fratribus per hunc modum repertus est predixisse. Scitote me nunquam nisi per manus infidelium moriturum: et non dubitetis quin mediolani me oporteat sepeliri. Sed nec de suo metuebat premio qui sic de merito certus erat. Sciens enim cui crediderat non impudenter. sed confidenter. sicut post bella uictoriam. sic coronam
10 sibi post uictoriam arrogabat: ut firmiter speraret et crederet quod adhuc nominaretur in letaniis et quod festum suum in kalendariis scriberetur. O beatum uirum. cui ex presenti uita iam futura inceperat. et cuius pedes iam in celestis ierusalem atriis stantes erant: et qui adhuc in carne corruptibili positus iam glorie incorruptibilis et
15 laudis perpetue primitias pregustabat.

de tractatu et predicatione mortis eiusdam

Porro uir sanctus preuidens propinquam sue terminum passionis; acceptum mandatum summi pontificis: tanto instantius atque constantius exsequi cepit quanto de reliquo repositam sibi cernebat coronam iustitie. in illum diem a iudice iusto esse reddendam. uerum

---

19 comites fieri] *transp. A* | consentirent] no break *P1 P2 P3 Ty Tr Ps S F N W Nv*
III.iii,1 Insuper] *add.* beatus petrus *TA* | pro…suam] uitam suam pro fide *S*
2 accepit] accepterat *TA* hac fuit *Taeg* | fideliter] fidenter *TA Taeg* | et] quam *A*
Taeg **3** prophetico spiritu] *om. TA* **4** etiam] *om. TA* **5** modum] mundum *exp.* et
corr. modum *P3* **6** nunquam] *add.* pro *P3* | non] ne *P1 P3 Ty Tr* **7** mediolani]
mediolanum *P1 P3 Ty Tr* **8** crediderat] dederat *P3* | non…9 sed] *om. TA* nec
imprudenter sed *Taeg* **10** speraret] saperet *A Taeg* | speraret…crederet] crederet et
speraret *P3* | et] ac *S F Ps N W* **11** quod…suum] *om. TA add.* etiam *T* | suum]
om. P3 **12** O…15 pregustabat] *om. TA* **13** pedes] *om. P3 Tr* | ierusalem atriis]
transp. P1 P3 Ty Tr | atriis] *add.* pedes *P3 Tr* **14** et¹] *om. Taeg* **15** pregustabat]
degustabat *Taeg* | pregustabat] *add.* xviii *P1* **16** de…eiusdam] om *P1 P3 Ty Tr*

frequently offered to throw himself into the fire to prove the truth of the faith, if only the heretics would consent to be his companions there.

In addition to this, he was eager to offer his life for the faith, not only   III.iii
by exposing it to danger, but also by his death. Perhaps this was by a divine revelation, for he mentioned it often as if in a prophetic spirit. One time he spoke about his blessed martyrdom and also the place of his burial, and he foretold both of these things to the brethren, "Know I will not die save at the hands of the infidels, and do not doubt it, in fact it is fitting for me to be buried in Milan." But neither did he dread his reward, of which he had merited the knowledge. For knowing Him in whom he believed, not shamelessly but confidently as after a victory in battle, so he claimed the crown after his triumph. He firmly knew and believed that he would be named in the litanies and that his feast would be inserted in the calendar. O blessed man, who has already begun the future life in this present one, and whose feet already stand at the gate of the heavenly Jerusalem! He who till now was in corruptible flesh, yet has already tasted the glory of incorruptibility and the first fruits of never-ending praises.

On the method of his death and of his preaching about it.   III.iv

Seeing in advance how near he was to the day of his passion and, having received the command of the Supreme Pontiff, he began to execute his office with vigor, since he saw the crown of justice laid up for him on that day when the just Judge would grant it. Moreover the

---

III.iii,1 In…III.v,21 the²] Taegio, 4.30; LA 425.   **17** …III.vi,10 confessing] Taegio, 4.30; LA 425.   **III.iv,1** Seeing…III.iv,1 day] LA, 425; and Bull of Canonization

---

TA | et predicatione] *om.* Ps | predicatione] predictione W | eiusdam] cuiusdam P2 *add.* xviii capitulum N **III.iv,1** uir sanctus] *transp.* P3 | preuidens] prouidens A **2** atque…3 constantius] *om.* F S Ps N W TA **3** exsequi] exequi TA *Taeg* cepit] *add.* atque constantius F S Ps N W **4** iudice iusto] *transp.* Ps N TA F *al. man. sup. corr.*

5 uidentes et dolentes heretici negotium fidei per christi pugilem sic
uehementius prosperari; de ipsius morte cum suis fautoribus tractare
ceperunt. arbitrantes se posse pacifice uiuere. si eorum tam ualidus
persecutor de medio tolleretur. Nec latuit sanctum tractatus occultus
hostium. ex certis relationibus plurimorum; sed ipse uelud pugil
10 intrepidus. nec metuebat quod dudum desiderio ardenti sitiuerat. nec
in eo quod confidenter inceperat tepescebat: sciens quod occidi
poterat. sed minime uinceretur occisus. unde dominica in ramis
palmarum. quatuordecim diebus felix eius precedente martyrium;
apud mediolanum coram copiosa populi multitudine. predicauit se
15 certum fore. quod heretici mortem suam tractauerant. et quod pro
ipsa iam erat pecunia in deposito constituta; sed agant inquit quod
uoluerint. quia plusquam uiuus fecerim faciam mortuus contra eos.
assignato autem quibusdam hereticorum fautoribus usque ad octauas
pasche termino peremptorio. quo precise mandatis parerent ecclesie.
20 predicens se in eodem termino reuersurum. ad cumanam ciuitatem
profectus est: ubi prioris inter fratres suos officio fungebatur.

5 et dolentes] *A Taeg* | per…pugilem] pro christi pugile *Pı P3 Ty Tr* | sic] *om. TA*
6 suis fautoribus] *transp. TA*   **9** uelud] ueluti *Taeg*   **10** nec[1]] *om. Ty add. al. man.*
sup. | desiderio ardenti] *transp. TA Taeg*   **11** confidenter] fidenter *A* | tepescebat]
represcebat *A* retardabat *Taeg*   **13** palmarum] *add.* xiiii *Pı Tr* xiii *P3* | eius
precedente] presciens eius *Tr* | precedente] presciens *Pı P3 Ty* precedentibus *N*
14 populi] *om. TA* | populi multitudine] *transp. S F Ps N W Tr Taeg*
15 tractauerant] tractauerunt *A Taeg*   **16** ipsa] ipso *A Taeg* | pecunia] pecuniam *Pı*
m *exp. om. S* | quod] quidquid *Tr*   **17** uoluerint] *add.* quod *Ps* | uiuus] unius *Ps*
cancell. *al. man. dex.* uiuus | faciam mortuus] *transp. P2 S F Ps N W TA Taeg*
19 peremptorio] parentorio *W*   **20** in…termino] termino in eodem *Ps* | termino]
add. mediolanum *TA* | cumanam] cumana *A* comensem *Taeg*

heretics, seeing they were suffering pain since the work of the faith strongly prospered under the champion of Christ, began to discuss the deaths of him and his associates, considering whether they would be able to live peacefully if they could remove such a strong persecutor from their midst. Nor did the secret plans of the evildoers lie hidden from the saint, for he received many reliable reports, but like a brave warrior he neither feared anything, since formerly he had thirsted with an ardent desire for martyrdom, nor did he delay what he had confidently begun, knowing that he was able to be killed but – having been killed – that he would conquer. Therefore on Palm Sunday, the fourteenth day preceding his happy martyrdom near Milan, he was preaching in the presence of a great multitude. He preached that the heretics contemplated his death, and that money was laid in deposit for the crime. He said, "Let them do what they wish. I will be worse to them in death than in life." He allotted a delay to certain *fautores* of heresy until the end of the octave of Easter, during which time they had to obey the command of the Church foretellling that he would have returned within that same period of time, and he departed for Como, where he was the prior of the brethren.

_____

14 Therefore...24 brethren] VF, 239   **20** fautores...heresy] A *fautor* was a term used by the inquisition to denote anyone who aided heretics in any way, it did not always denote someone who was actively committed to heresy, but it was a punishable offence.

de passione eius et morte

Anno domini mcclii die sabbati quod est finis septuagesime quodque sabbatum in albis et annotinum pascha uocatur; athleta christi de conuentu suo ad pugnam fidei mediolanum rediens: satagebat datum terminum peruenire. Cumque medium iter carperet; quidam funestus
5 hereticus. et crudelis hereticorum satelles. eorum inductus precibus et pretio quadraginta librarum conductus: in sanctum uirum iter salutaris propositi prosequentem. In agnum utique lupus. ferus in mitem. in pium impius. furibundus in mansuetum. in modestum effrenis. profanus in iustum. sacrilegium presumit insultum. exercet
10 conatum. mortem intentat. et de sacerdote faciens uictimam. sacrum illius caput crudeliter impetens scelerato mucrone. et sauciato sanguine iusti ense: geminatis et diris in ipso impressis uulneribus. non diuertentem ab hoste. sed exhibentem se protinus hostiam. et occisoris sustinentem in patientia truces ictus. in loco passionis
15 prostratum seminecem dereliquit. et ad fratrem dominicum ipsius comitem. aerem miserandis uocibus adimplentem inuocando auxilium. mox ille carnifex se conuertens: quatuor letalibus eum uulneribus sauciauit. cui dum percussiones ita crudeliter inculcaret; uir sanctus ex parte altera suum domino commendans spiritum: In
20 manus inquiens tuas domine commendo spiritum meum. a fidei

---

III.v,19 In … 20 meum] Lk 24:46

---

22 de … morte] de uenerando triumpho passionis eius *TA*   de passione et morte *Ps* om. *P1 P3 Ty Tr* | morte] *add.* xix capitulum *N* xix *Ps*   **III.v,1** Anno] *add.* itaque *TA* | Anno … III.v,1 die] igitur *Taeg* | mcclii] *add.* octauo ydus aprilis. *TA* m. ducentesimo. lxxo quodque *P3 exp.* | sabbati] sabbato *A Taeg* | quod] qui *A Taeg* finis septuagesime] *transp. Taeg*   **2** sabbatum] sabbato *A* | de … 3 suo] de ciuitate cumana ubi fratrum sui ordinis prior erat: *TA*   **3** fidei] *om. A Taeg*   **4** peruenire] *add.* pro exequenda inquisitione contra hereticos sibi ab apostolica sede commissa. *TA* | medium iter] *transp. P1 P3 Ty Tr* | funestus … 5 precibus] et de ipsorum hereticorum credentibus prece inductus illorum *TA* qui locus est juxta Barlasinam, ad sinistrum loci latus, in nemore denso, funestus ille Carinus, hereticus et crudelis hereticorum satelles, eorum, ut dictum est, inductus precibus *Taeg*   **6** sanctum uirum] eum *TA*   **7** prosequentem] *add.* funestus insilit *TA*   **8** mitem] *add.* in mite *S exp.*   **9** effrenis] effrenus *Tr P3* effren *P1* us *sup.* | iustum] sanctum *T* sanctum *P1*

On his passion and death III.v

Therefore Saturday (which is the end of the seventy days, called *Sabbato in Albis*, in reference to the preceding feast of Easter) the athlete of Christ was returning to the battle at his convent in Milan, but instead came to the end of his life. When he was in the middle of his journey, a violent heretic and cruel follower of heretics, had been hired at their request for the price of forty *lire*, and it was he who sped the holy man in the journey of salvation. It was like a sheep against a wolf, the meek one against a savage, the pious against the impious, the tame against the raging, the modest against the unrestrained, the just against the profane. Threatening death, he made a victim of the priest, then throwing himself at that sacred head with his accursed sword, he sated it on the blood of the just one, repeatedly hacking at his wounds. Peter, not turning from the enemy, immediately showed himself as an offering, and patiently suffered the awful blows of the murderer. Laid low in the place of his suffering, he was half-dead. Suddenly the butcher turned to Fra Domenico, his comrade who was filling the air with calls for help from his pitiful voice, and gave him four lethal wounds. In response to the crude blows, the holy man for his part commended his spirit, saying, "Into your hands, O Lord, I commend my spirit." (Lk 24:46) He did not even then cease to

---

25 ...III.viii,5 faith] Taegio, 4.30; LA 425. **III.v,1** Therefore...III.v,29 martyrdom] LA, 426-427; Taegio, 5.38. | the[1]...2 Albis] Durandus, the medieval authority on liturgical matters, considered that the names of the numbered Sundays (i.e. Septuagesima) were to be counted from the octave of Easter rather than from Easter itself, so the Saturday after Easter was seventy days after Septuagesima Sunday.

---

exp. | sacrilegium] *om. TA Taeg* **10** intentat] intenta *A Taeg* | et...uictimam] *om. TA* | sacrum] *add.* autem *TA* **11** crudeliter] *om. A Taeg* | mucrone] *add.* diris in ipsum impressis uulneribus *TA* **12** iusti] uita *A om. P3* | geminatis...uulneribus] uenerandum illum *TA* **13** hostiam] *add.* deo *A Taeg* **14** occisoris] cesoris *T* | in[2]] *add.* ipso *TA* **15** et] Moxque *TA om. P3* **17** mox] *om. TA* | letalibus eum] *transp. P3* illum lethalibus *Taeg* **18** crudeliter] letaliter *T* crudeles *Taeg* **19** ex] in *P1 P3 Ty Tr* | commendans spiritum] spiritum commendabat dicens *T* commendat spiritum *Taeg* **20** a...21 desistens] *om. T*

preconio etiam in hoc articulo non desistens. symbolum fidei quod propter blanditias auunculi puer disseri noluerat. propter mortis angustias. uelut preco fidei nequaquam oblitus est confiteri: prout ipse nephandus fuge fraudatus presidio postmodum a fidelibus captus. ad

25 clamores fratris dominici excitatis et dictus frater dominicus diebus aliquibus superuiuens: postea retulerunt. Sed cum adhuc martyr domini palpitaret. cultellum crudelis lictor arripuit; et per latera totaliter confitentis transfigens: beatum eius martyrium consummauit.

Sicque finita huius peregrinationis septuagesima: felix uiator celestem uenit ad patriam. Sic stolam suam martyr et uirgo dealbauit in albis: sic ad eternum sabbatum celebrandum exsabbato temporali migrauit; pascha enim annotinum suo agno non caruit: quandoquidem petrus

5 in eo: tanquam agnus innocens immolatus. in ipsa die sui martyrii simul confessor. martyr. propheta et doctor quodam modo esse promeruit. dum ipso die confessione more solito facta. deo sacrificium laudis optulit: et fidem christi constanter inter tormenta confessus. ueram fidem edocuit. clara uoce cum pateretur symbolum

10 fidei profitendo. pro defensione fidei sanguinem suum fudit. confessorum doctorum et martyrorum se numero sociauit.

Prophetarum uero meruit adiungi collegio. prophetico spiritu predicens quod contigit. Cum enim tunc ipse quartanam pateretur

---

III.vi,2 dealbauit…albis] Apoc 7:14

---

21 symbolum] *add.* quoque *T* **22** propter[1]…23 confiteri] *om. T add.* cepit dicere, cuus in hoc articulo propter mortis angustias desiit esse preco *T* | auunculi] patrui *Taeg* **23** prout] ut *Ps* **24** postmodum] *om. T* | captus] *add.* fuit *T* | ad…25 excitatis] *om. T* **25** dictus] prefatus *T* | frater] super *P3* **26** cum] dum *Taeg* **27** crudelis lictor] *transp. T* **28** totaliter] taliter *P2 F Ps N W om. P3 Taeg* totaliter *Ty exp.* to | consummauit] *add.* octauo die aprilis *T no break P1 P2 P3 Ty Tr Ps S F N W Nv* **III.vi,1** Sicque] sic itaque *TA Taeg* | huius] huiusmodi *P1 Ty* celestem…2 patriam] uenit ad celestem patriam *TA* **3** exsabbato] exsabbati *P1* **4** quandoquidem] quidem *P3 add.* sanctus *T* | petrus] *om. Taeg* **5** tanquam] tamquam *Taeg* | immolatus] immolatur *Taeg* | sui martyrii] *transp. T* **6** simul] *om. P3* | propheta] *add.* simul *T* **8** laudis] *om. T* | optulit] obtulit *T Taeg*

proclaim the faith, nor did he forget to confess the creed, which he had not abandoned as a boy even at the coaxing of his uncle, like a herald of the faith even in the pangs of death. The wicked killer, cheated in flight, was captured later by one of the faithful who had been roused by the cries of Fra Domenico, and the brethren later related that they brought back Fra Domenico, who survived for some days. But when the Martyr of the Lord stirred one last time, the cruel killer took his dagger and stabbed the confessor in the side. In this way he consummated his blessed martyrdom.

So having finished his Septuagesimal pilgrimage, the happy traveler came to his native land. The martyr and virgin made white his garment; (Apoc 7:14) he went from the temporal Saturday to the eternal Sabbath. The preceding Easter did not lack its lamb, seeing that in Easter week such an innocent lamb was offered up. In that day of his martyrdom, he merited to be confessor, prophet, martyr, and doctor, all at the same time since on that day, having followed his usual habit of confession, he offered the sacrifice of praise, and having constantly confessed faith in Christ during his torments, he taught the true faith by confessing the creed in a clear voice, even while suffering. For the defense of the faith he poured out his blood and united himself to the number of confessors, doctors, and martyrs.

III.vi

He had merited to be added to the company of the Prophets, for by a spirit of prophecy he foretold what happened. Since he was then

III.vii

III.vi,1 So...IV.i,5 faith] Taegio, 4.30; LA 425. | So...III.vii,16 them] Taegio, 5.39. **3** from...4 Sabbath] Tommaso is playing with the name of the feast on which he was martyred, Sabbato in Albis. **12** confessors...martyrs] In reference to the *Te Deum laudamus*. **III.vii,1** He...IV.ii,1 day] Taegio, 4.30; LA 425.

---

constanter...tormenta] inter tormenta constanter *Taeg* **9** cum] *om. P3* **10** profitendo] *add.* et *Taeg* | defensione] *add.* siquidem *P1 exp.* | fudit] *add.* et sic *P1 exp.* fuditur *P3* ur *exp.* **11** sociauit] no break *P1 P2 P3 Ty Tr Ps S F N W Nv* **III.vii,1** collegio] consortio *Taeg* **2** tunc ipse] *transp. P3* | ipse quartanam] ipse cartanam *TA* quartanam *Taeg*

dicentibus sociis quod non possent illa die mediolanum applicare:
respondit si ad domum fratrum non potuerimus peruenire: apud
5   sanctum simplicianum poterimus hospitari. quod et factum fuit. nam
cum eius sacrum corpus mediolanum in plaustro a fratribus
deferretur; lictore capto uel in uincto sequente. fama tanti facinoris
uolans uelocius ac mediolanum perueniens: urbem totam subuertit
populorum tumultibus. et concursu. quem potestas mediolanum.
10   metu noue turbationis attonitus: clausis ianuis ciuitatis non potuit
impedire. quin tanta foret plebis occurrentis impressio. quod
archiepiscopus etiam cum suo clero et religiosis quam plurimis. sancto
martyri processionaliter occurrentes: uix ad corpus pertingere
ualuerunt; propter quod et fratres non potuerunt illud eadem die ad
15   domum deducere. sed apud sanctum simplicianum depositum.
ibidem assistentibus fratribus illa nocte remansit.

Illud quoque in hoc loco pretermittendum non est. quod martyrium
huius sancti sollempnius efficit: et martyr aliorum martyria indicat
gloriosum nam eius passio ueneranda: passionis christi propinqua
prefert ymaginem. nempe christus pro ueritate fidei quam docebat.
5   petrus pro ueritate fidei quam defendebat bibit calicem passionis.
christus passus est ab infideli populo iudeorum: petrus ab infideli
turba hereticorum. christus in paschali tempore crucifigitur: et eodem
tempore petrus occiditur. christus cum pateretur in manus tuas
domine commendo spiritum meum dicebat: petrus eadem uerba cum
10   occideretur clamabat. christus pro triginta denariis fuit traditus ut
crucifigeretur: petrus pro quadraginta libris papiensium fuit uenditus
ut interficeretur. christus per passionem multos ad fidem adduxit.

---

3 applicare] applicaret *P3*   **5** et] *om. P1 P3 Ty*   **6** a] *om. Taeg* | a...7 deferretur]
deferretur a fratribus *T*   **8** ac] *om. Taeg* | perueniens...9 mediolanum] *om. S add.*
al. man. subscr. | subuertit] commouit *N Taeg*   **9** populorum tumultibus] populi
tumultus *P2* | concursu] *add.* ita *T* | quem] quod *T* | quem...mediolanum] adeo
ut qui preerat mediolano. *Ty* | potestas] portarius *P1* pretor *Taeg* | mediolanum]
mediolanensis *Ps W N T Taeg*   **10** ciuitatis] *om. Tr add. al. man. dex.*   **14** ualuerunt]
potuerunt *P1 P3 Tr Ty* | propter...15 deducere] propter quod fratres eadem die ad
domum illud deducere non poterunt *Taeg* | fratres] *add.* apud *corr. N* | eadem...
15 domum] ad domum eadem die *P1 P3 Ty Tr* ad domum suam eadem die *T*
16 remansit] *no break P1 P2 P3 Ty Tr Ps S F N W Nv*   **III.viii,1** martyrium...3

suffering from quartan fever, his companions suggested that he might not make it to Milan. He responded, "If we are unable to get to the house of the Brethren we will be able to lodge at San Simpliciano." And so it was. For when his holy body was carried in a cart to Milan by the brethren, the murderer having been captured and led in chains, news of the great outrage flew swiftly, reaching Milan. The whole town was in an uproar at the confusion of the assembled populace. The podestà of Milan, fearing of a new disturbance, was unable to keep the gates of the city closed. There was such an onrush of people, with the archbishop with his many clergy and religious running to meet the procession of the Holy Martyr. Even they were scarcely able to reach the body. Because of this the Brethren were unable to bring the body home that day, but laid him in San Simpliciano, where it remained that night attended by them.

One should also not overlook the place that the martyrdom of the saint was brought about. This holy man showed forth the glories of the Passion of Christ in his own death. Of course, Christ suffered for the truth of the faith that He taught; Peter drank the cup of suffering for the truth of the faith which he defended. Christ suffered on account of the infidelity of the Jewish people, Peter because of the infidelity of the mob of heretics. Christ was crucified at Paschaltide, and in that same period Peter was also killed. Christ, while He suffered, said, "Into your hands, O Lord, I commend my spirit," Peter uttered those same words when he was killed. Christ was handed over to be crucified for thirty pieces of silver, Peter was sold for forty Pavian *lire* so that he might be killed. Christ led many to faith by His passion, Peter converted many heretics by his death. But although this

III.viii

---

3 quartan fever] Likely a type of parasitic malaria. **III.viii,1** One…IV.iii,5 voice] Taegio, 4.30; LA 425. | One…30 power] LA, 426-427; Taegio, 5.40.

---

gloriosum] *om. T* **2** sancti] *om.* Ps W | martyria] martyrium *Taeg* **3** gloriosum] gloriosa P1 P3 Ty Tr | propinqua] propinquam *T Taeg* **4** nempe christus] *transp. T* **7** tempore] turba *exp.* P1 *corr.* tempore *al. man. marg. sup.* **9** domine] *om.* P3 **10** occideretur] pateretur Ps **11** fuit uenditus] *transp. Taeg* **12** christus…fidem] *om.* P3

petrus per mortem multos hereticorum conuertit. Quamuis enim
fidei pugil egregius. hereticorum dogma pestiferum plurimum
15   eradicasset in uita: post mortem tamen eius intercedentibus meritis. et
crebris miraculis coruscantibus fuit a deo extirpatum: ut quam
plurimi errorem suum relinquerent. et ad sancte gremium ecclesie
conuolarent. ita ut ciuitas mediolanensis et comitatus eiusdem ubi tot
hereticorum conuenticula residebant. adeo sit purgata ut expulsis aliis.
20   aliisque ad fide conuersis nullus ibidem auderet aliquatenus apparere;
plures etiam ex eis heresiarche maximi et famosi ordinem
predicatorum ingressi: hereticos et fautores eorum usque nunc feruore
mirabili persequuntur. Sic sampson plures philisteos occidit moriens:
quam uiuens occiderat. sic granum frumenti cadens in terra.
25   infidelium manibus mortificatum. uberem consurgit in spicam. sic
botrus in torculari compressus: liquoris redundat in copiam: sic
aromata pilo contusa: odorem plenius circumfundunt. sic granum
synapis attritum uirtutem suam fortius demonstrauit.

IV   *de miraculis diei mortis eius et primo de curatione fistule*

Ceterum post sancti uiri gloriosum triumphum. celi rosario dudum
clauso per petri martyrium reserato. celestia miracula crebrius
refulserunt: quibus dominus suum martyrem illustrauit. Terra enim
suo sanguine roseo madidata. uberiores fructus protulit. quos celo
5   cum letitia intulit. preconis fidei et martyris christi suffulta suffragiis.

III.viii,23 Sic...24 occiderat] Jdg 16: 23–31

---

14 hereticorum] *om. Taeg*   **17** gremium ecclesie] *transp. T*   **18** ita...20 conuersis]
om. T   **19** aliis] *om. P2*   **20** nullus] *add.* quia *T* | ibidem auderet] *transp. T*
21 ex...22 ingressi] ex eis heresiarche magni et famosi heresi penitus abiurata
predicatorum ordinem sunt ingressi *T* ex his, heresiarche pessimi et famosi,
Ordinem Predicatorum ingressi *Taeg*   **22** ingressi] *add.* qui postmodum *T*
fautores eorum] *transp. T* | usque...23 persequuntur] ufuerunt feruore mirabili
persequiti *T* mirabili feruore persecuti sunt *Taeg*   **23** persequuntur] consequuntur
P3 | sampson] sanson *S F W*   **24** sic...28 demonstrauit] *om. T*   **26** botrus] petrus
P1   **28** demonstrauit] *add.* xx *P1 add.* potestate domino nostro ihesu christo. cui
honor est et gloria in secula seculorum. Amen. Explicit uita et passio sancti petri

distinguished fighter rooted out many a pestiferous teaching during his life, nevertheless after his death, by the merits of his intercession and frequent demonstrations of miracles, error was rooted out by God to such a great degree that very many abandoned their heresy and flocked to the bosom of the holy Church, so much so that the city and county of Milan, where there were a number of heretical conventicles, were purged in such a great degree that some were expelled and others were converted to the faith, and would never dare to appear again. Also many famous and powerful heresiarchs entered into the Dominican order, and heretics and their supporters were pursued with a marvelous fervor. Thus Samson killed more Philistines in death than he had slaughtered while living (Jdg 16: 23–31); thus the grain of seed, falling to earth, put to death by the hands of the unfaithful, arises as a plentiful ear of corn; thus the grapes, crushed in the winepress, overflow into a multitude of juice: as aromatic spices having been crushed by a pestle, abound in the fulness of scent; thus the mustard seed having been ground, shows forth its strong power.

On the miracles of the day of his death, and firstly the cure of fistula.   IV.i

After the glorious triumph of the saint, the closed rose garden was opened through Peter's martyrdom, the heavens glittered with many miracles through which the Lord gave glory to His holy martyr. The earth wettened by his rosy blood yielded rich fruit, which He sent from heaven with joy, by the merits of the herald of faith and the martyr of Christ. In diverse parts of the world and in various

---

martiris ordinis predicatorum *Ty* **29** de[1] ... fistule] *om. P1 P3 Tr TA* | diei] dici *S corr. al.* man diei | eius] *om. P2* | fistule] *add.* xx capitulum *N* xx. *W* **IV.i,1** post] *om. P2* | sancti uiri] sancti Petri martyris *TA transp. P1* | uiri] *om. TA Taeg* celi ... 7 rutilare] *om. T* **3** suum] sanctum suum *Taeg* **4** sanguine] cruore *Taeg*

que in diuersis orbis partibus pluribusque prouinciis. per signorum
euidentiam non desinunt rutilare. Quorundam quedam licet summus
pontifex in suis litteris breuiter refereat comprehensa. nos tamen
quantum possumus signorum ordinem prosequentes. et ad
10 edificationem legentium et audientium latius describenda
prouidimus. adiciendo nichilominus alia que postmodum attestione
fidelium uerissime sunt comprobata; hoc denique prelibato. quod
miracula plura facta sunt. quam probata et scripta. multa etiam sunt
causa uitande prolixitatis obmissa. quedam uero que congrue tacere
15 non poterant inferius annotantur.

de muliere fistulose curata.

Eodem namque die sue passionis et mortis. quedam infirma nomine
iacoba. ad corpus sancti accedere auida. sed per longum temporis
spacium. ex pressura confluentis multitudinis non permissa. ut sue
infirmitatis reperiret auxilium. quod a medicis destituta nequiuerat
5 optinere: tandem uix in ecclesiam beati simpliciani. ubi corpus iacebat
martyris introducta. super caput suum de quo propter morbum fistule
iam plura ossa perdiderat. manu martyris faciens sibi fieri signum
crucis: plenum sanitatis beneficium adipisci promeruit.

IV.i,8 comprehensa … 15 annotantur] Included in Surius, IV, 692. "quorum etsi
nonnulla summus Pontifex suis litteris strictius comprehenderit; et nos tamen quoad
possumus miraculorum ordinem consequenter, ad lectorum et auditorum utilitatem
latius distribuimus; alia quedam adiicientes, que postea fidelium hominum
testimoniis uerissime sunt approbata: ubi tamen hoc premissum uolumus, plura esse
edita miracula quam sint in scripta redacta, multa etiam prolixitatis uitande causa
pretermissa: pauca autem que tacere noluimus iam commemoramus."

---

6 orbis] mundi *Taeg*   **7** rutilare] *add.* miraculis *Taeg* | Quorundam] quorum *T*
8 pontifex] *add.* innocencii *T* | suis … breuiter] littera canonizationis eisdem *T*
breuiter refereat] *transp.* P2 S F Ps N W | refereat comprehensa] comprehendit
dicens. *T* | comprehensa] *add.* etiam P2 *exp.* | comprehensa … 15 annotantur] *om.*
T Taeg   **10** describenda] distribuenda P1 P2 P3 distinguenda *Tr* scribenda *N Nv*
11 prouidimus] *add.* et P1 *exp.* | alia] *exp.* P1   **12** uerissime] *om.* Ps W | uerissime
sunt] *transp.* P3 | comprobata] *add.* et P1   **13** plura … sunt[1]] sunt plura facta P3
14 que congrue] *transp.* P3   **15** annotantur] *add.* xxi P1   **16** de … curata] *om.* P1 P3

provinces his glory did not cease to shine by evident signs. Although the Supreme Pontiff referred briefly to certain of these in his letters, still we are able to follow their order more completely and, for the edification of those who read and hear, we have taken care to describe more completely and to add other things which afterwards were proven more fully by the witness of the faithful, and will at length be examined, for many more miracles were done than were proven and recorded, and many are also omitted for the sake of avoiding wordiness, but some others however which it is not appropriate to pass over in silence, are noted below.

On the cure of a woman with a fistula IV.ii

On the day of his passion and death there was a sick woman by name of Jacoba who was eager to approach the body of the saint in order to receive some help for her infirmity which she had been unable to obtain, having been abandoned by the doctors. She was not able to approach the body for a long time because of the press of the populace. At last, she came into the church of San Simpliciano with difficulty, where the body of the martyr lay. She caused the dead martyr to make the sign of the cross over her head, in which many bones had been lost on account of her fistula, and she merited to obtain the benefit of complete healing.

IV.i,7 Although ... 9 completely] This seems to indicate that Thomas Agni had access to the *inquisitio in partibus* records which are now lost, and elaborates Innocent's brief mentions with many other pre-canonization miracles. **IV.ii,1** On ... IV.ii,10 healing] Taegio 5.40.

Tr TA de curatione fistule *P₃* de muliere fistulosa *N* | fistulose] fistulosa *W* curata] xxi capitulum *N* xxi. *W* **IV.ii,2** iacoba] *add.* cum *P₁ P₃ Tr* **4** reperiret] recipiret *Taeg* | nequiuerat] poterat *T* **6** introducta] *add.* et *P₁* | super] *om. T* suum] *add.* indinata *P₁ exp.* **7** faciens ... fieri] sibi faciens *P₁ P₃ Tr* **8** adipisci promeruit] *transp. T* | promeruit] *add.* xxii *P₁*

de reuelatione et curatione monialis apud florenciam.

Eodem die etiam in monasterio dominarum de ripolis. iuxta
florentiam posito. dum quedam sanctimonialis in oratione persisteret;
aliquantulum soporata. uidit beatam uirginem in excelso throno in
gloria residere: et duos fratres predicatores in celum ascendere. et hinc
5   inde iuxta eam collocatos esse. Et cum mirans quereret quis nam
essent: uocem sibi respondentem audiuit. hic est frater petrus
ueronensis: qui in conspectu domini tamquam fumus aromatum
gloriosus ascendit. Quod a significatione non uacat. quod frater
dominicus qui uisus est cum eo celum ascendere: non tamen cum eo
10 auditus est nominari. nam qui secum passus. secum celum creditur
ascendisse: non tamen secum fuit in cathalogo sanctorum ascriptus.
Dicta igitur soror fama postmodum docente cognoscens. quod una
eademque die. cum sancti martyrio sua uisio concurrebat; statim
sumpta fiducia martyri se deuouit: et deuotis meruit precibus a
15 quadam infirmitate antiqua subito liberari. sicque reuelationis ueritas.
concordia temporis et adeptione miraculosa salutis. tamquam
argumento duplici est probata.

de lampadibus frequenter celitus accensis ad sepulcrum.

Ut autem fidelium tristitia. ex subtractione tanti propugnatoris exorta.
noue lucis ortu plenum uerteretur in gaudium. lampades ad
uenerabile sepulcrum. martyris in ecclesia beati eustorgii dependentes:
pluries per seipsas absque omni humano studio et ministerio diuinitus

---

9 de…florenciam] de muliere fistulosa curata *Ps* *om.* *P1 P3 Tr TA* *add.* xxii
capitulum *N* xxii *W* **IV.iii,1** Eodem…IV.iii,1 die] *transp.* *T* **2** sanctimonialis]
testimonialis *S* testi *exp.* **3** soporata] *add.* est. et *P1* | throno] trono *P1* h *sup.*
5 eam collocatos] eam collocatos *P3 exp. add. al. man. dex.* collocatos | quis nam]
qui nam *S F Ps N W Taeg* **6** essent] esset *P1 P3 Tr* | frater] om *P1 P3* **7** fumus]
add. an *P3 exp.* **8** significatione] *add.* rationis *P1* | non] *add.* pone *P3* | frater]
super *P3* **9** qui] *add.* uus *P3 cancell.* **10** celum] *add.* ascendere; non tamen cum eo
P3 exp. **11** in] *om.* *F S Ps N W* | ascriptus] adscriptus *Taeg* **13** cum] est *P3* | sua]
om. *T* **14** deuotis] deuote *P3* | deuotis…precibus] *om.* *T* **16** adeptione] adeptio
ne *P1* ne *exp.* | salutis] sanitatis *Taeg* **17** est probata] comprobata est *Taeg*
probata] *add.* xxiii *P1* **18** de…sepulcrum] De reuelacione et curatione monialis

Of the vision and cure given to a nun at Florence

IV.iii

On that same day in the monastery at Ripoli, near Florence, a certain nun stood praying, though she was slightly sleepy. At length she saw the Blessed Virgin on a high throne in glory, and two Friars Preachers ascending into heaven, who were placed on either side of her. And when seeing this she asked who then they might be, she heard a voice replying, "This is Friar Peter of Verona, who has arisen as a glorious aromatic offering in the sight of the Lord." Even so Fra Domenico, who was seen to ascend to the heavens with him, was nevertheless not named with him. For he who suffered with him is also believed to have ascended into heaven with him but nevertheless was not added to the catalog of the saints. The sister, later learning of the martyrdom, found out that her vision occurred on the same day. She immediately vowed herself to the martyr and merited by her devout prayers to be instantly relieved from a certain old infirmity. The truth of the vision was thus proven by a two-fold argument, since it agreed in the time it took place and was demonstrated by the miracle of healing.

Of the lamps that were frequently lit at his tomb

IV.iv

So that the sadness of the faithful – arising from the absence of so great a defender – might be fully turned to joy by the illumination of new lights, the lanterns hanging over his venerable tomb in the church of Sant'Eustorgio were lit frequently by divine ministrations,

---

IV.iii,1 On…IV.iii,17 healing] LA 437; VF, 437; Taegio 5.41. **IV.iv,1** So… IV.iv,15 both] Bull of Canonization; Taegio, 5.42.

---

apud florenciam *Ps (note: Ps mixes titles for the next few stories.) om. P1 P3 Tr* sepulcrum] *add.* xxiii capitulum *N* xxiii *W* **IV.iv,1** Ut…IV.iv,2 gaudium] Post mortem uero ipsius *TA* | tristitia] *add.* ex *Taeg* | ex] *om. P1* **3** uenerabile sepulcrum] speculum eius uenerabile *T* | martyris] eius *Taeg* | martyris… dependentes] *om. T* | beati] sancti *Taeg* **4** omni] *om. Taeg* | diuinitus] *om. P1 P3 Tr Ty*

5 sunt accense. quia conueniens nimis erat. ut qui igne ac lumine fidei excellenter claruerat: singulare de ipso ignis et luminis miraculum appareret. Super locum etiam passionis eius. sepe luminaria de celo descendentia. et ad celum ascendentia: plures religiosi. aliique quam plures uisibiliter conspexerunt. inter que luminaria: duos fratres in
10 habitu predicatorum se uidisse testati sunt. Sic namque sanctitati martyris congruebat; ut frequens lux de celo descendens. nunc lampades nunc pro lampadibus aerem inflammans. euidentius appareret: et ubi sacrum corpus est conditum. et ubi sanguis innocens est effusus. Et sicut lumen multoties exortum est. sic utrobique multa
15 diuina miracula claruerunt.

de curatione triplicis morbi in eadem persona.

Ex quibus illud euidens et mirificum taceri non debet. quod in quodam paupere mediolanensi. qui dicebatur iacobus de cornaredo. aperte monstratum est. Nam cum haberet sinistre manus digitum. ex morbo fistule in septem locis plurimorum foraminum concauitate
5 defossum; alterum etiam pedem uehementi tumore deformem et eiusdem pedis tibiam carnibus defluentibus putrefactam. ita quod uix ad aliquem locum. in quo a transeuntibus peteret elemosinam poterat proficisci: nisi sub ascellis suis duobus baculis sustentatus. audito quod per nouum martyrem tot beneficia prestarentur: spe
10 consequende sanitatis. adiutus ad sepulcrum sancti qualitercumque peruenit. ubi oratione fusa cum lacrimis: sensit se subito liberatum. Digiti namque sui foramina sunt obstructa. et mira consolidatione sanata; pes tumorem deposuit: ac tibia proiecta putredine. cicatrice

---

5 sunt] super *P3* | quia] *add. al. man. dex. P1* | conueniens] *add.* eius *P1 exp.* erat] fuit *Taeg* | qui] quam *T* **6** excellenter claruerat] *transp. P1 P3 Tr* **7** eius] eiusdem martyris *T* **8** ad...ascendentia] ascendentia ad celum *Taeg* | celum] *om. P3* **13** et¹] tam *T* | est conditum] *transp. T Taeg* | et²] *add.* quam etiam *T* **14** est¹] *om. S F Ps W* | est effusus] *transp. Taeg* | effusus] *add.* sic *P3 exp.* | sicut] sic *P1 P3 Tr add.* utrobique *P2 F S Ps N W* | sicut...est²] *om. P1 Tr* | lumen...sic] *om. P3* | exortum est] *transp. N* | utrobique] *om. T* **15** claruerunt] *add.* xxiiii *P1* **16** de...persona] de lampadibus frequenter celitus accensis ad sepulcrum *Ps om. P1 P3 Tr TA* | eadem] una *W* | persona] *om. P2 add.* xxiiii capitulum *N* xxiiii *W* **IV.v,1** Ex...**IV.v,2** qui] quidam nempe pauper mediolanensis dictus *TA* **2** paupere]

without the care or attendance of anyone, so that he who was marvelously illuminated by fire and the light of faith might be shown forth by the singular sign of fire and light. Also, over the place of his passion many religious and lay people often saw a light descending from heaven and rising back up to heaven, and they testified that two in the habit of the Friars Preachers were often seen. This corresponds to the holiness of the martyrs, that in the place where the holy body was laid out or where innocent blood was shed there might frequently appear a light coming down from heaven, or a lamp being lit, or the air setting the lamp alight. And where the light shone in both places, so many divine miracles were likewise worked in both.

On three illnesses cured in the same person.

IV.v

Among all these things, we ought not to be silent about the evident and wondrous cure that was plainly shown in a certain pauper of Milan called Jacopo da Cornaredo. The fingers of his left hand suffered from a fistula which was digging a cavity there in seven different places, further he also had a deformed foot with a terrible tumor, and the flesh on his foot and leg had begun to decay, so that when he appeared in any place to beg for charity from passersby he was unable to leave unless supported by two crutches under his arms. Hearing that the new Martyr excelled at giving aid, he came with difficulty to the Saint's tomb with the hope of eventual health. There, praying with flowing tears, he felt himself healed. His fingers were removed from the cavities and the holes were wondrously filled in and healed, the tumor disappeared from his foot, and his shine – which

7 Also … 10 seen] LA, 427 **IV.v,1** Among … IV.v,16 function] Taegio, 13.101.

pauperes *P3* s *exp.* | dicebatur] *om. Taeg* | cornaredo] *add.* dicebatur *Taeg* **3** aperte … cum] *om. T* **4** morbo fistule] *transp. P1 P3 Tr* **5** et] *om. P3* **7** peteret elemosinam] *transp. Taeg* | poterat … 8 proficisci] *transp. Taeg* **8** nisi] ubi *P3* ascellis] acellis *P2 T* asellis *N* axillis *Taeg* | suis] *om. Taeg* | duobus baculis] *transp. Tr* | sustentatus] substentatus *P3 F* **10** adiutus] *om. Taeg* | sepulcrum sancti] *transp. Taeg* **11** peruenit] uenit *Taeg* | oratione fusa] *transp. P3* | subito] *om. Taeg*

salutifera est obducta. Et sic qui prius operari. nec ambulare nequibat;
15   ad utrumque potens factus est et ydoneus membrorum suorum
officiis restitutus.

De curatione apostematis fistulosi.

In persona etiam cuiusdam ymilie papiensis simile miraculum
manifeste resplenduit. nam postquam osculata est martyris
monumentum. statim curata est a quodam apostemate fistuloso:
clausis. xi. foraminibus. per que sanies eiusdem apostematis dudum
5   effluere non cessabat.

De curatione cancri corrodentis carnem.

Sed nec illud minus euidens fuit. quod gestum est in quadam
belsauere mediolanensis diocesis. cuius carnes cancer edax annis
pluribus sedula corrosione uorabat. que cum ad locum fuisset delata
martyrii. uulnera sua confricans terra sanguine martyris rubricata;
5   non solum tunc nouo dolore caruit. que ibi pannorum tactum non
ualebat antea sustinere: quin potius ab antiquo dimissa uelocem et
integram consecuta est uirtute innocentis sanguinis sanitatem. qui
quidem non solum egros liberabat a morbis: sed etiam a mortis ianuis
morituros.

De suscitatione pueri cadentis.

In mortis enim discrimine positus quidam puer papiensis. nomine
conradinus. cum inter trabes acutas grauiter corruisset impulsus; et ex

---

14 operari nec] *om. Taeg* | nequibat] non poterat *Taeg*   **15** potens] petens *P3*
17 De…fistulosi] *add.* xxv *P1 add.* xxv capitulum *N Note P1 P3 Tr begin headings*
here de curatione triplici morbi in una persona *Ps* | fistulosi] fistule *W* **IV.vi,4** xi]
xi undique *Taeg*   **6** De…carnem] De curatione apostematis fistule *Ps add.* xxvi *P1*
P3 F add. xxvi capitulum *N* xxvi. *W* **IV.vii,1** Sed] *add.* nec *Taeg* | Sed…IV.vii,1
illud] *om. P3* | nec] *om. P1* | nec…minus] illud uero uarios *Tr* | illud] *add.* non
P1 | fuit] est *P1 P3 Tr* | est] fuit *P1 P3 Tr* | quadam] *add.* muliere *Taeg*
2 belsauere] blasancte *P1 P3* blasanete *Tr om. Taeg*   **5** que ibi] quem ibi *Taeg*
tactum] tactu *Taeg* | non²…6 sustinere] sustinere antea non poterat *Taeg* **6** ab] pro
P1 P3 Tr | dimissa] dimisso *P1 om. Taeg*   **7** integram] *add.* sanitatem *Taeg*

showed through the rotting flesh – was covered over by a healing scab. He who before was unable to walk, was given the ability and his members were restored to their proper function.

On the cure of a fistulous abscess IV.vi

A similar miracle was recorded in Pavia for a woman named Emilia. After kissing the Martyr's monument, she was immediately cured from a certain fistulous ulcer that had eleven holes, which before had not ceased to flow with a bloody pus.

On the cure of a flesh-eating cancer IV.vii

But that miracle was no less evident than one done for a certain Belsavere of the diocese of Milan, whose flesh a rapacious cancer had devoured for many years with unyielding vigor. When she had come to the place where the martyr had been killed, rubbing her wounds on the ground reddened by the blood of the martyr, not only was she then freed from any new pain, but since before she had not been able to tolerate the touch of cloth (a condition which afflicted her for a long time) she was restored to health completely, by virtue of the innocent blood. Peter's blood did not only deliver the sick from their illnesses, but also those at the point of death.

On the cure of a boy who had fallen IV.viii

A boy from Pavia named Conrad was near death, having been struck when running between sharp stubs of treetrunks, and was so painfully

---

IV.vi,1 A…IV.vi,4 pus] Taegio, 13.101. **IV.vii,1** But…IV.vii,10 death] LA, 428; Taegio, 5.43; Bull of Canonization. **IV.viii,1** A…IV.viii,7 friends] LA, 428; Taegio, 5.43; Bull of Canonization.

---

sanitatem] *om. Taeg* **8** sed] *add.* reuocabat *P1 P3 Tr* | ianuis] ianua *P1 P3 Tr* portis *Taeg* **10** De…cadentis] *om. P1 add.* xxvii *P1 P3 F W add.* xxvii capitulum *N* **IV.viii,1** In…IV.viii,1 positus] *om. Taeg* | nomine…2 conradinus] *transp. Taeg* **2** conradinus] curradinus *S Nv* corradinus *N* coradinus *W*

casu fuisset grauissime sic oppressus: ut motu et sensu penitus
destitutus. tanquam mortuus a matre tristissima defleretur; mox
apposito de terra suo pectori eiusdem martyris sacro cruore contacta.
sic incolumis resurrexit: quod iam matrem iocundam deferens.
gaudens abiret protinus cum suis sociis ad ludendum.

de gutta sanata per terram sanguine martyris rubricatam.

Preter hec autem plura sunt alia non supprimenda silentio; que in
ciuitate et dyocesi mediolanensis. et propinquis regionibus. tum in
loco passionis. tum ad sepulcrum martyris. tum ad eius memoriam
facta sunt: mira et uaria miracula coruscarunt. quandam enim
uiduam nomine miranam. in parochia sancti prothasii mediolanensi
morantem: super leoneto filio suo. uirtuosus sanguis martyris
mirabiliter letificauit. Cum enim puer quadam gutta ita grauiter. xx.
mensibus fuisset afflictus: quod dorsi eius nodi uiderentur per tumore
ac doloribus dissoluendi. propter quod futurus gibbosus a medicis
credebatur; mater locum doloris. terra perfusa martyris cruore liniuit:
et filio protinus liberato extra domum exiliens. uicinas conuocat et
amicas. ut sibi super salute filii congauderent.

de graui morbo febriuum per eandem

Aliam preterea mulierem. sabinam nomine de lugano cumane
diocesis. a medicis ex acumine febrium desperatam; terra solummodo

4 tristissima defleretur] plangeretur *Taeg* 5 apposito] apposita *Taeg* | de] *om. Taeg*
eiusdem] eius *P3 add. al. man. dex.* dem | sacro] *om. Taeg* | contacta] consecrata
Taeg 6 incolumis resurrexit] uiuus et incolumnis resurrexit *Taeg* | resurrexit]
exsurrexit *P1 P3 Tr* | matrem] *add.* reddens *Taeg* | deferens] *om. Taeg* 8 de...
rubricatam] *add.* xxviii *P1 P3 F W add.* 28 capitulum *N* **IV.ix,1** Preter...IV.ix,4
coruscarunt] *om. T Taeg* | hec autem] *transp. P3* | que] qui *P's* 2 regionibus] rep.
P3 3 eius] *add.* ad *P3 exp.* 4 quandam] quamdam *Taeg* | enim] *om. Taeg*
5 sancti prothasii] SS. Gervasii et Protasii *Taeg* 6 leoneto] leonasio *P3*
7 mirabiliter] *om. Taeg* | puer quadam] *transp. P1* | ita] tam *Taeg* | xx...8
mensibus] *om. Taeg* 8 dorsi] *add.* et *P3 exp.* | nodi] *add.* et *P3 exp.* 10 locum

overwhelmed by the accident, that he lost sense and motion, and he was most piteously mourned by his mother as if he were dead. When dirt consecrated by the blood of the martyr was placed on the wound, he arose living and unharmed, and leaving his joyful mother, and gladly went back to playing with his friends.

On the cure of arthritis by earth reddened by the martyr's blood IV.ix

Besides these there are many others which cannot be consigned to silence, which were done in the diocese of Milan and in neighboring territories, not only at the place of his passion and at his tomb, but also happened to those making remembrance of him. A widow by the name of Mirana, a resident of the parish of SS. Gervase and Protase, rejoiced marvelously regarding Leoneto her son because of the most powerful blood of the martyr. Once the boy was seriously afflicted with terrible arthritis for twenty months (on account of which great knots appeared on his back which were loosened only with great pain and swelling). Because it was so serious physicians believed that he would henceforth have a hump. His mother smeared the painful spot with the ground stained by the blood of the martyr. On account of her son's healing, she burst forth from the house and called together friends and neighbors so that they might congratulate her son on his healing.

Of a grave fever healed by the same earth IV.x

A woman named Sabina from Lugano in the diocese of Como, having been despaired of by the physicians because of an acute fever,

---

IV.ix,4 A...15 healing] Taegio, 5.44.   **IV.x,1** woman...5 health] Taegio, 5.43.

---

doloris] *transp. Taeg* | liniuit] perfusa siniuit *Taeg*   **11** conuocat...12 amicas] *om. Ps*
12   congauderent] congratularentur *Taeg*   **13**   de...IV.xii,7 ueritatem] *om. Tr*
eandem] *add.* curato. xxix. *P1 P3 F W add.* terram sanato xxviiii capitulum *N*
IV.x,1   Aliam...IV.x,1 preterea] *om. Taeg* | mulierem] *add.* quandam *Taeg*
cumane] comensis *Taeg*   **2** febrium] febris *Taeg*

super quam martyr christi interfectus fuerat liberauit: et super faciem
febricitantis aspersa: ipsam perfecte restituit sanitati.

de scrophula disparente per eandem

In eadem uilla puella quedam nomine iacobeta. cum propter
quamdam scruphulam nucis magnitudinem excedentem. alterum
brachiorum haberet non modicum deformatum. auditis beneficiis per
martyrem suum a christo exhibitis. prostrata in terram. et obsecrans
quod sicut eum uere sanctum fore credebat. sic eam dignaretur
dominus liberare: ita fuit miraculose curata ut infra triduum.
scruphule quam per decennium gestauerat. nec ullum uestigium
remaneret.

de liberatione confracti et contracti

In alia etiam uilla episcopatus eiusdem. que dicitur surgum. cum
quidam nomine leonastius. de domo episcopi comensis sic confractus
fuisset et contractus; quod nullo sibi medicine adminiculo suffragante.
per sex annos sine duobus sustentaculis nequiuerat ambulare; emisso
uoto ad martyrem; ad martyris monumentum sine aliquo
sustentaculo liberatus accessit. ubi persoluens quod uouerat. cum
quattuor sociis sub iuramento testatus est miraculi ueritatem.

---

3 super¹] supra *Pɪ* | quam] qua *Taeg* | martyr...fuerat] interfectus fuit martyr
christi *Pɪ P3* | christi] *om. S add.* ut *S exp.* | super faciem] faciei *Taeg* 5 de...
IV.xi,8 remaneret] *om. Tr* | scrophula] scrufula *W* | eandem] *add.* xxx. *Pɪ P3 W*
add. xxx capitulum *N* **IV.xi,1** In...IV.xi,1 quedam] de Lugano Comensis diocesis
Taeg | uilla] *add.* p *P3 cancell.* | nomine iacobeta] *transp. Taeg* 5 sanctum] *add.*
fore *Taeg* | fore] *om. Pɪ P3* | eam dignaretur] *transp. Pɪ* 6 curata] sanata *Taeg*
add. est *exp. Pɪ* 7 scruphule] scrufule *W* scofulis *Taeg* | quam] quas *Taeg* | ullum]
ullius inueniret *Taeg* 8 remaneret] *om. Taeg add.* laudans Deum in sancto Martyre
suo *Taeg* 9 de...IV.xii,7 ueritatem] *om. Tr* | confracti...contracti] contracti et
confracti. xxxi *Pɪ P3 add.* xxxi *F W add.* xxxi capitulum *N* **IV.xii,1** alia...surgum]
diocesi Comensi apud a Suricam villam super lacum Larium *Taeg* 2 leonastius]
leonasius *P3* Lemasius *Taeg* | comensis] *add.* de alto corruens *Taeg* 3 et contractus]
om. Taeg | nullo] nullus *Taeg* | medicine adminiculo] *transp. Pɪ P3* | adminiculo
suffragante] adminiculis suffragantibus *Taeg* 4 sex] sex ui *Pɪ* uii *P3 corr.* ui

was freed merely by passing over the land on which the Martyr had been killed, and sprinkling the dirt on her feverish face, she was restored to perfect health.

Of scrofula that vanished by application of the same earth IV.xi

A girl of Lugano in the diocese of Como named Jacobetta had a small deformity on one of her arms – larger than the size of a nut – on account of scrofula. Hearing about the gifts bestowed by Christ through His Martyr, she prostrated herself on the ground beseeching that just as she believed him to be a true Saint, so might the Lord deign to free her. She was so miraculously cleansed that within three days the scrofula was gone, and not the least trace of the deformity which she had borne for ten years could be found.

Of the freeing of those who were constricted in body IV.xii

In the diocese of Como at the village of Sorigo there was a man name Leonasio of the household of the Bishop of Como. He was so fractured and constricted that the physicians were unable to aid him in any way, and for six years he was unable to walk without two crutches. Having uttered a vow to the holy Martyr, he went to Peter's tomb freely without the aid of any crutches. There he fulfilled his vow and, with four companions, he testified to the truth of the miracle under oath.

IV.xi,1 A…IV.xi,8 found] Taegio, 13.102. **IV.xii,1** In…IV.xii,9 dropsy] Taegio, 13.99.

---

nequiuerat ambulare] ambulate nequiret *Taeg* **5** martyrem] *add.* et *P1 add.* sanctum *Taeg* | martyris monumentum] ipsius tumulum *Taeg* **7** sub] cum *Taeg*

de curatione cuiusdam ydropice

Quedam quoque mulier dicta cara de lignano sic grauata et tumefacta
erat morbo ydropico. quod ad sancti tumulum uix adduci ualuit aut
portari: fusa tamen oratione ibidem. grauitate prorsus ac tumore
depositis. sic protinus est curata. ut facta leuis ac gratilis. per se libere
5   et ire potuit. que prius alterius adminiculo portabatur.

de curatione contracte que perdiderat usum lingue

Sed et alia quedam nomine uindis. de ualle leuentina mediolanensis
dyocesis. cum totius sinistri lateris longo tempore usu carens surgere
de lecto nequiret. facto voto deo et martyri. se ad eius ituram
tumulum et manum et pedem cereum oblaturam. si sibi liberationis
5   remedium contulisset: protinus liberata. illius patrie gentem. flere pre
gaudio et admiratione coegit.

de curatione alterius habentis manuum arefactam.

Simili fecit totam uiciniam admiratione letari quedam paralitica
nomine agatha; que dum uenetiis uno latere perdito. in domo
cuiusdam matrone de parochia sancti johannes in bragola. duobus
annis et dimidio sustentata decumberet; metuens ne hospite sue. et

---

8 ydropice] *add.* xxxii. *P1 P3 F W add.* xxxii capitulum *N*   **IV.xiii,1** quoque] uero
P1 Tr add. uero *P3 al. man. sup. om. Taeg* | dicta] *om. Taeg* | de lignano] nomine,
de Lignano Mediolanensis diocesis *Taeg*   **2** erat morbo] *transp. Taeg* | sancti] *add.*
Petri *Taeg* | adduci] duci *F S Ps W* | adduci…3 portari] portari potuit aut duci
Taeg   **3** tamen] autem ibidem *Taeg* | prorsus…4 depositis] omni et tumore
deposito *Taeg*   **4** facta] *om. Taeg* | gratilis] *add.* facta *Taeg*   **5** ire…portabatur]
expedite ire poterat, que prius alterius adminiculo portabatur. *Taeg* | potuit]
potuerit *F S Ps N W*   **6** lingue] *add.* xxxiii. *P1 P3 F W add.* xxxiii *N*
IV.xiv,1 Sed…IV.xiv,1 alia] *om. Taeg* | Sed…IV.xiv,7 arefactam] *om. Tr* | nomine]
quedam mulier nomine *Taeg* | uindis] uiridis *F S Ps N W Nv* | mediolanensis…2
dyocesis] *transp. Taeg*   **3** et] *add.* eius *Taeg*   **4** et manum] *om. Taeg*   **7** alterius] *om.*
P1 | arefactam] *add.* xxxiiii. *P1 P3 F W add.* xxxiiii capitulum *N*   **IV.xv,1** Simili]

On the cure of one who had dropsy   IV.xiii

There was a woman named Cara of Legnano, who was so burdened and weighed down by the illness of dropsy that she was scarcely able to be carried or led to the tomb of Saint Peter. But when she arrived there, pouring forth her prayers, she was cured straightaway of all sickness and tumors, so that she was made light and graceful, and she was able to leave quickly under her own power, who a little before had been carried in with assistance.

On the cure of a woman who was paralyzed and who had lost the ability to speak   IV.xiv

A woman named Vinde of the Valle Leventina in the diocese of Milan was unable to get out of bed for she had been without the use of her left side for a long time. She vowed to God and to His Martyr to make a journey to his tomb and offer a waxen foot if he would bring her a remedy of deliverance; immediately she was freed, and she called to her family weeping for joy and wonder.

On the cure of another who had a withered hand   IV.xv

A similar miracle brought wonder and joy to all bystanders regarding a woman named Agatha who was a paralytic in Venice and who had lost the use of one side of her body. When she had lain in the house of a certain matron in the parish of San Giovanni in Bragora for

---

IV.xiii,1 There...IV.xiii,7 assistance] Taegio, 12.92. Bull of Canonization; LA, 428. Both Bull and *Legenda* say it was at the place of the martyrdom, not the tomb. **IV.xiv,1** A...IV.xiv,6 wonder] Taegio, 13.99.   **4** waxen foot] Body parts formed in wax, especially those that were the subject of the healing, were common *ex voto* offerings at shrines.   **IV.xv,1** A...IV.xv,30 Milan] Taegio, 12.96.

---

add. modo *Ps* | Simili...IV.xv,2 nomine] mulier quedam *Taeg*   **2** agatha] *add.* nomine *Taeg* | que...uenetiis] paralitica Venetiis fuit, que *Taeg* | perdito...3 de] *om. P3* | in...3 matrone] cuiusdam matrone domo *P1 Tr*   **3** cuiusdam...bragola] dum in quodam domicilio cujusdam matrone, in parochia S. Joannis in Bragola *Taeg*   **4** et[1]] cum *Taeg* | et dimidio] *om. P3*

5   aliis que sibi manum misericordi porrigebant. nimis honerosa fieret et
uerteretur in tedium. eo quod ad sedendum se erigere saltem dum
comederet non ualeret: ut ad quoddam hospitale deferretur. multis
precibus impetrauit. ubi hospitalarium non reperiens hospitalis; ad
priorem locum necessario reportata. desolata nimium et afflicta: tribus
10   diebus adiutorium noui martyris. cui se deuouerat expectauit. Quarta
uero feria diescente quemdam fratrem predicatorem soporata
conspexit; qui se medicum asserens ipsius manum que iuxta lectulum
arida dependebat accepit. promittens ei beneficium plenarie sanitatis.
At illa excitata pre gaudio et quod sibi promissum fuerat sentiens
15   adimpletum. tunicellam sibi porrigi a quadam muliere petiuit. Dum
autem uelut sana se libere indueret. et leta se miraculose diceret
liberatam: altera mulier hec uidens et audiens. prestolari donec foret
induta stupore miraculi stimulata non potuit: quin statim ad
dominam domus properans. ei sanatam fore agatham nunciaret.
20   Ceterum dum illa stupefacta currit ut uideat. et iam hec induta
occurrit ut obuiet; concurrit tota uicinia a predicta muliere
circumquaque commota: et sic undique deo et martyri multiplices
gratie referuntur. Que autem beneficium salutis acceperat; uerborum
solummodo gratias non contenta referre; manum misit ad fortia. et
25   fusum nuper sanatis digitis apprehendens. duas purpuras processu
temporis adquisiuit. unam uenetiis ad altare martyris offerens. alteram
mediolanum ad tumulum eius transmittens.

---

5 manum misericordi] *transp. Taeg* | fieret] haberetur *P1 P3 Tr* esset *Taeg*
6 erigere] accingere *Taeg* | saltem] *om. P1 P3 Tr*   **7** ualeret] ualebat *Taeg*
multis…8 precibus] *transp. Taeg* **8** hospitalis] hospitalem *S N W* hospitale *F P2 P3*
om. Taeg **9** reportata desolata] *transp. P3* | desolata] *add.* et *P3 exp.*   **11** soporata]
reportata *P2 exp.*   **12** manum] *add.* quod *P3 exp.* | que] *add.* lecto *Tr* cancell.
lectulum] lectum *P1 P2 P3 Tr*   **13** promittens…sanitatis] beneficium plenari
sanitatis beneficium ei promittens *Taeg*   **14** et] *add. marg. sin. P1*   **15** porrigi] *om.*
P1 P3 Tr   **16** miraculose…17 liberatam] diceret miraculose sanatam *Taeg*
17 foret…18 induta] *transp. P1 P3 Tr*   **19** nunciaret] nuntiauit *Taeg add.* cum *P3*
exp.   **20** Ceterum] *om. Taeg* | iam hec] *transp. Taeg*   **21** occurrit] concurrit *Taeg*
22 undique] auide *Taeg* | multiplices…23 gratie] *transp. Taeg*   **23** beneficium
salutis] sanitatis beneficium *Taeg*   **24** non…referre] referre non contenta *Taeg*
manum] *add.* suam *Taeg*   **25** fusum…sanatis] *om. Taeg* | digitis] *add.* nuper sanatis

two-and-a-half years, fearing that her hostess and others who had extended their hands in mercy would become exceedingly burdened with her and might, out of weariness, turn her out (since when she sat to eat, she was unable to arise), she began to beseech them to take her to some hospital. When, not finding a hospital, she was carried back to the first place out of necessity, and not a little desolate and afflicted she hoped and prayed three days for the help of the New Martyr, to whom she was devoted. On the fourth day she saw a certain Friar Preacher in her sleep who, declaring himself a doctor, took her hand which hung limply at the side of her bed and promised her the benefit of complete health. At these words, excited beyond all joy, and feeling the promise fulfilled, she asked another woman to bring out her tunic. And when she was clothed in it she felt herself healthy and free, and she happily told of the miracle that freed her. Another woman saw and heard this and waited until she was covered, and in a stupor and excited by the miracle, hurried to the lady of the house to whom she gave the news of Agatha's healing. Dumbfounded, she ran and saw that the one in the tunic was already rushing to meet her. They ran into each other nearby, and the other women were completely shaken, excitedly giving many thanks to God and the Martyr. She who had received the gift of health, not contented with only giving words of thanks, put forth her strong hand with its recently cured fingers and took two silver coins which she had acquired over the course of time, and offered one at a Venetian altar dedicated to the holy Martyr, and sent the other one to his tomb in Milan.

---

27 two … coins] "duas purpuras" probably indicates Byzantine money used then at Venice.

---

fusum *Taeg* **26** altare] *add.* sancti *Taeg* **27** mediolanum] mediolani *Taeg* tumulum eius] *transp. Taeg* | transmittens] mittens *Taeg*

de liberatione cuiusdam demoniace

Non solum autem in curatione morborum sed in expulsione
demonum plurimum energuminorum sanatio: potestatem a deo
martyri traditam demonstrat apertius. Nam matrona quedam nomine
gerolda. uxor jacobi de ualle sana. cum. xiiii. annis ab immundis
5 spiritibus fuisset obsessa: ad quemdam sacerdotem ueniens dixit. Ego
sum demoniaca: et spiritus malignus me uexat. Mox sacerdos territus
fugiens. sacristiam intrauit; et librum quemdam in quo erant
coniurationes demonum et stolam latenter sub capa deferens: cum
bona societate ad mulierem rediit. Quem mox ut uidit. ait; latro
10 pessime quo iuisti? Quid est quod sub capa occulte portasti. Cum
autem sacerdos adiurationes suas faceret et nil curationis afferret.
uenit illa ad beatum petrum dum adhuc uiueret. ab eo postulans
adiuuari. Cui ille prophetica uoce respondit age inquiens penitentiam.
confide filia ne desperes. quia etsi id quod postulas perficere ad
15 presens non ualeo: tempus tamen adueniet. quo a me id quod petis
plenarie optinebis. Quod et factum est. nam post passionem eius ad
sepulcrum martyris ueniens. liberationem ab infestatione demonis

---

28 liberatione] curatione *Ps* | demoniace] *add.* xxxv. *P1 P3 F W add.* xxxv
capitulum *N* **IV.xvi,1** Non … IV.xvi,3 Nam] *om. Taeg* | in¹] *add.* purgatione et *P1*
P3 Tr | sed] et in *Ps* | in²] *om. P1 P2 P3 Tr* **2** sanatio] sanitatem *P1* sanitas *P3 Tr*
sanatione *N* sanatione *F exp.* e **4** gerolda] geralda *P1 P3 Tr* Girolda *Taeg* | ualle
sana] ualle sanata *P1 P3* ualle sanatum *Tr* Valesina *Taeg* | xiiii annis] *transp. P3*
5 sacerdotem ueniens] *transp. Taeg* **6** me uexat] *transp. Taeg* **7** sacristiam]
sacristinam *S* | erant … 8 demonum] coniurationes demonum erant *Taeg* **8** sub
capa] *om. P1 P3 Tr* **9** Quem] que *Taeg* | ut] *add.* eum *Taeg* **10** Quid … portasti]
om. Taeg **11** suas] *om. Taeg* | nil] nihil *Taeg* **12** petrum] *om. P3* | postulans … 13
adiuuari] *transp. Taeg* **13** uoce] *om. P3* | age … penitentiam] *om. Taeg* **14** id] *om.*
P2 F S Ps N W Taeg | id quod] quid *F* **15** tempus … adueniet] tamen ueniet
tempus *P1 Tr* cum ueni et tempus *P3* tempus tamen ueniet *N W* | me] *add.* petis
P3 exp. | id] *om. Taeg* | petis … 16 et] *om. S add. al. man. subscr.* **17** sepulcrum
martyris] *transp. Taeg* | liberationem … demonis] ab infestatione demonis
liberationem *P1 P3 Tr*

On the freeing of a certain demoniac   IV.xvi

The power of God worked through the martyr was plainly shown not only in the healing of the sick, but also in the expulsion of many demons from those who were possessed. A matron named Girolda, the wife of Jacobo di Valle Sana, had been possessed by an unclean spirit for fourteen years and, coming to a priest, she said, "I am a demoniac, and an evil spirit troubles me." Suddenly the terrified priest ran into the sacristy where the books for exorcism of demons were kept and he secretly placed his stole under his cappa and returned with good fellowship to the woman. When she saw him she said, "Evil thief, where did you go? What is it that you are wearing hidden under your cappa?" But when the priest began to make adjurations and nothing produced a change, she came to Blessed Peter, who was then living, asking him for assistance. To her he responded with a prophetic voice, "Do penance! Trust, daughter. Do not despair, because although what you ask I am unable to do for the present, the time draws near when you may obtain all that you ask from me." And so it was: for after his passion she came to the tomb of the Martyr to obtain liberation from the demonic infestation promised by the living Peter, and she completely obtained it from the dead Peter, although with much vomiting of blood.

IV.xvi,3 A…20 blood] Taegio, 14.111.

promissam a uiuo. licet cum multo uomitu sanguinis optinuit a
defuncto.

de liberatione alterius.

Alia quoque nerbona nomine de bethegno. a demonibus possessa sex
annis possessoribus renitentibus uelut armatis fortibus custodientibus
atrium suum: ad sacri corporis tumulum uix est tracta. Qua ibidem
cum multa difficultate detenta: de uno detinentium qui erat credens
5   hereticorum. conquerebantur demones et dicebant. Tu qui noster es
quid nos detines? et ut eum confundendo repellerent: ipsius occulta
crimina publicabant. Nonne dicentes te ad illum locum et illum
duximus ubi peccata talia et talia commisisti? Denique obsidentes
obsessam ut meritis martyris coacti desererent mulierem multum
10   discerpentes: quasi mortuam reliquerunt. Predictus uero incredulus
corradus de ladriano uocatus. qui ad hoc uenerat ut sancti miracula
derideret: attendens quod uere demones erant illi. sicut suorum
conscii secretorum: et ille uere sanctus. qui tales taliter expellebat: per
uiam mirabilis misericordie ad lumen conuersus est ueritatis.

V   *de diuersis curatis*

Quid plura? Plures alios obsessos a demonibus. eiectis illis de
corporibus liberauit; febres expulit. languidos plurimos et diuersis

---

18 cum...sanguinis] multa sanguinis effusione perfecte *Taeg* | multo] magno *P1 P3
Tr* **20** liberatione] uratione *Ps add.* cuiusdam *N* | alterius] *add.* xxxvi *P1 P3 F W
add.* xxxvi capitulum *N* **IV.xvii,1** nerbona...bethegno] Herbona de Befegro *Taeg*
bethegno] befegro *P1 Nv* betegno *Tr* bethegro *N* bethtegno *W* | possessa...2
annis] possessa vi. annis *P1* sex annis possessa *Ps* possessa annis sex *F* obsessa sex
annis *N* annis sex possessa *Taeg* **4** detinentium] detenetium *Taeg* | erat...5
hereticorum] hereticorum credens erat *Taeg* **5** conquerebantur] colloquebantur
Taeg **7** publicabant] *add.* dicentes *Taeg* | Nonne] *add.* nos *Tr* | dicentes] inquiunt
P1 Tr nos inquiunt *P3 om. Taeg* | ad...locum] *om. Ps* | locum] *om. P1 P2 P3 F S
N W* | et illum] *om. Ps exp. P1* | illum²] *add.* locum *P1 P2 P3 F S N W* **9** meritis
martyris] *transp. P1 P3 Tr* | meritis...10 discerpentes] eam desererent coacti,

On the liberation of another IV.xvii

Another woman, Nerbona de Befegro, was possessed by demons for six years, and these demons were like strongly armed men guarding a palace, so she was dragged to the tomb where the holy body lay. With much difficulty she was detained there by a man who was a believing heretic. The demons wailed and asked, "You are one of ours, why do you detain us?" So that they could drive him away in confusion, they tried to make public some hidden sin of his saying, "Have we not led you to that place, where you committed such and such sins?" Finally they attacked the possessed woman. In order to get them to depart from her, he made an oath by the merits of the Martyr, and the woman seemed like she was dead and, almost tearing her to shreds, the demons left her. The incredulous one, called Corrado de Landriano, who had come there to deride the miracles of the saint, seeing that there truly were demons, felt guilty because of the secrets revealed and was awed by the true Saint who had so mightily driven away the demons, and he was led by the wondrous mercy of God and converted to the light of Catholic truth.

On different cures

What more is necessary? He freed many others obsessed by demons by casting them out of their bodies, he drove out fevers, and many

---

IV.xvii,1 Another … IV.xvii,17 truth] Taegio, 14.111. | Befegro] Possibly Bettegno, near Pontevico in the province of Brescia.

---

meritis Martyris adjurati, mulierem quasi mortuam, multum eam discerpentes *Taeg* | martyris] *om. Ps* **11** corradus] Conradus *Taeg* | ladriano] landriona *N* Landriano *Taeg* **12** quod] add de. *P3 exp.* | illi] *om. Taeg* | sicut] sic *Taeg* **13** uere] uerus *Taeg* | tales] *om. P1 P3* | taliter] *om. Tr* | expellebat] *add.* tales *P1 P3* taliter *Tr* **14** uiam] *add.* misericordie *P3 exp.* | misericordie] *add.* Dei *Taeg* est] *add.* Catholice *Taeg* **15** curatis] *add.* xxvii *P1 sic add.* xxxvii *P3 F W add.* xxxvii capitulum *NN* **V.i,2** languidos] langidosque *Ps W* languidesque *N*

infirmatibus occupatos. qui etiam sepulcrum eius in uehiculis et aliis sustentaculis adierunt. exinde postmodum plena incolumitate recepta: sine aliquibus subsidiis. laudantes dei clementiam. ad propria redire concessit.

de correctione detractoris per adhesionem morselli et curatione eiusdem.

Porro illud dignum memoria tacere non congruit; quod non tamen matryris sui deuotis. dominus curationis prestabat suffragium. sed etiam detractoribus correctionis beneficium adhibebat. unde cum quidam mediolanenses ciues. in commune prandentes de ipso ad inuicem litigarent; et unus eorum sanctitatem martyris et miracula protinus deprauaret. sumpto quodam sub attestatione morsello. quod eum non posset si circa hec falsum diceret transglutire: sensit mox ipsum suo gutturi sic herentem. ut illum educere uel inducere non ualeret. Quare illico penitens: et iam uultus mutato colore quasi sentiens uicine mortis euentum; facto intra se uoto quod linguam de cetero ad talia non laxaret: fuit protinus illo euomito liberatus.

de correctione alterius per subtractionem loquele et curatione eiusdem.

Sic apud florentiam quidam iuuenis heretica prauitate corruptus: cum in ecclesia fratrum de florentia. cum quibusdam aliis iuuenibus ante quamdam tabulam staret. in qua sancti petri erat depictum martyrium: lictorem percutientem martyrem gladio euaginato aspiciens in hec uerba prorupit: utinam ego ibi fuissem: quia ualidius

---

7 eiusdem] *om. P1 P3 Tr add.* xxxviii. *P1 P3 F W add.* xxxviii capitulum *N*
V.ii,1 Porro ... V.ii,3 adhibebat] *om. T Taeg* **3** unde] *om. T Taeg* | cum] *om. T*
cum ... 5 litigarent] Quidam autem cum uesceretur cum aliis *T* **4** prandentes]
comedentes *Taeg* | ad ... 5 inuicem] de Beato Martyre invicem *Taeg* **5** et unus]
unusque *Taeg* | eorum ... 6 deprauaret] et illius sanctitate et miracula deprauaret *T*
6 sub] *add.* hac *P1* | attestatione] obtestatione *T* | quod ... 7 transglutire] quod
eum non posset si circa hec delinqueret transglutire *T* quod eum deglutire non
posset si circa hoc falsum diceret *Taeg* **7** mox ... 8 ipsum] *transp. P3* **8** inducere]
intromittere *T* **9** illico] ille *T* **10** euentum] aduentum *P1 P3 Tr* **11** laxaret]
relaxaret *Taeg* | illo] eo *Taeg* **12** curatione] curationem *Tr* | eiusdem] *add.* xxxix.

who were weak and who suffered diverse sicknesses, and were brought to his tomb in carts or other forms of conveyance, were later fully restored to health, and were able to return home without the help of others, praising the mercy of God.

On the correction of a detractor by choking and then curing him V.ii

On the other hand, it is not right to keep silent because not only did the Lord furnish cures from prayers, but He also administered salutary correction to detractors. Two citizens of Milan whilst eating together were having a heated argument over Peter's sanctity. One of them immediately denigrated the Martyr's holiness and miracles; taking a mouthful he swore that he would not be able to swallow it if what he had said about the matter was false. He then felt his tongue cleave to his mouth, so much that nothing was able either to enter or leave it. At that moment he repented, and, though he turned red in the face and felt near death, he made a vow to himself that he would utter no ill words again with his tongue. He was immediately relieved by vomiting.

On the correction of another by depriving him of speech and then curing V.iii
him

At Florence a youth deceived by heretical depravity, stood with other boys in the church of the brethren at Florence before a picture of Saint Peter. Seeing the unsheathed sword by which the martyr was assailed, he erupted in these words, "Would that I had been there, I would have dealt a worse blow." Having said this immediately he was

---

V.ii,3 Two ... 12 vomiting] Taegio, 8.59. **V.iii,1** At ... V.iii,15 address] Taegio, 8.59; VF, 240; LA, 429-430

P1 P3 F W add. xxxix capitulum *N* **V.iii,1** quidam iuuenis] *transp. Taeg* | iuuenis] *add.* quidam *Taeg* | corruptus] deceptus *Taeg* **2** aliis] *om. Taeg* **3** erat ... 4 martyrium] martyrum erat depictum *P1 P3 Tr* depictum erat martyrium *Taeg* **4** lictorem ... 5 aspiciens] lictorem euaginato gladio martyrem percutientem prospiciens *Taeg* **5** fuissem] essem *P1 P2 P3 Tr*

percussissem. Quo dicto statim effectus est mutus. Cumque quid
haberet requisitus a sociis nichil eis respondere ualeret; dum ab ipsis
reducerentur ad domum. uidens in uia quamdam ecclesiam sancti
michaelis. de manibus sociorum elapsus intrauit ecclesiam: et flexis
10 genibus corde sanctum rogauit. ut sibi parceret; uoto sicut potuit se
obligans. quod si liberaretur sua confiteretur peccata: et omnem
heresim abnegaret. Tunc subito recuperata loquela. ad domum
fratrum ueniens: peccata sua confessus est heresi abiurata: dataque
licentia confessori quod hoc populo predicaret. Ipseque postmodum
15 in publica predicatione factum exurgens: coram omni multitudine
cuncta confessus est.

de correctione cuiusdam alterius

Alium quoque nobilem mediolanenses. sanctus a detractione correxit:
digitos ipsius obrigescere faciens; ut omnis homo timeret et omnis
lingua confiteretur catholice fidei ueritatem: et sui propugnatoris
uirtutum et signorum nequaquam magnalia deprauarent.

VI ### de canonizatione ipsius

Talibus autem rumoribus ad apostolicam sedem delatis. tantorumque
magnalium. summus pontifex per fide dignos pluribus intellectis.
exaltationi fidei et noui martiris congaudens preconiis: honori quoque
apostolice sedis congratulans. cuius inquisitorem et pugilem sic
5 mirificare dominus dignanter adiecerat; uirginalem eius innocentiam

---

6 effectus…mutus] factus est mutus *F* mutus effectus est *Taeg* | Cumque] Cum
Taeg **7** eis] *om. P1 Tr add. mar. sup. Tr* **8** reducerentur…domum] domum duceretur
Taeg | quamdam ecclesiam] *transp. Taeg* **9** elapsus] *add.* eam *Taeg* | ecclesiam] *om.*
Taeg **10** rogauit] *add.* Martyrem *Taeg* | parceret] indulgeret *Taeg* | potuit] *add.*
uoto *P1 exp.* **12** abnegaret] abiuraret *Taeg* | recuperata loquela] *om. Taeg*
13 fratrum] *om. S* | confessus…abiurata] abiurata heresi confessus est *Taeg*
heresi] *add.* ad *P3 exp.* **14** hoc] *add.* ipsum in *Taeg* | Ipseque] ipse quoque *P3*
postmodum] uero *Taeg* **15** factum] fratrum *P1 P3 Tr om. P2 Taeg* **17** cuiusdam]
om. P1 P3 Tr | alterius] *add.* xl. *P1 P3 F W add.* xl capitulum *N*
V.iv,1 mediolanenses] mediolanum *P1 P3 Tr* mediolanensem *N* **2** ipsius] *om. Taeg*
3 et] nec *P1 P3 Tr* **4** uirtutum] uirtutem *Taeg* | nequaquam] *om. P1 P3 Tr*

made mute. When his friends asked him what was wrong, and he was unable to reply, they led him home. On the way he saw a certain church of Saint Michael, and, escaping the hands of his comrades, he went into it; and kneeling before the sanctuary he begged the Saint to be lenient to him. He vowed, insofar as he was able, that if he were freed, he would confess his sins and abjure all heresy. Then, having at once regained his speech, he came to the house of the brethren, confessed his sins, renounced his heresy, and was given permission by the confessor to relate the incident to the public. Presently telling of what had happened in a public address, he laid bare all before the whole people.

On the correction of another   V.iv

Here is likewise another; the Saint admonished another noble Milanese detractor by making his fingers enlarge and stiffen, so that all men might fear and that all tongues might confess the truth of the Catholic Faith, and his power of defending it, and that the faithful might not be deprived of the wonder of a miracle.

On his canonization

Such stories of so many great wonders having reached the Apostolic See, made known by many worthy witnesses for the exaltation of the faith and for the praise of the new Martyr who brought honor to the Apostolic See, since the Lord had deemed its inquisitor and fighter worthy of glorification, that the pope ordered a diligent inquiry be

---

V.iv,1 Here … V.iv,5 miracle] Taegio, 8.59.   **VI.i,1** Such … VI.i,28 translation] Taegio, 6.45.

---

magnalia] miracula *Tr*   **5** ipsius] *add.* xli. *P1 P3 F W add.* xli capitulum *N*
VI.i,1 Talibus … VI.i,1 rumoribus] Crebrescentibus itaque per totam Italiam per merita B. Petri Martyris evidentibus miraculis *Taeg* | Talibus] *add.* iocundus *TA* tantorumque … 2 magnalium] *om. Taeg*   **2** pontifex] *add.* innocencius quartus *TA Taeg* | per] *add.* plures *Taeg* | pluribus] *om. TA*   **3** et noui] nouique *Taeg*
4 congratulans] aggratulans *P2 F S Ps N W*   **5** uirginalem] *add.* quoque *exp. P1*

fecit studiose discuti. Et suorum copiam meritorum sollerter inquiri: miraculorum quoque gloriam diligenter examinari. precedentem et sequentem sue triumphalem titulum passionis. Et quia manifeste cognouit super excrescentiam ueritatis ad famam. cum sibi minora

10 quam reperit insinuata fuissent. de communi consilio cardinalium et prelatorum omnium qui tunc apud sedem apostolicam residebant. viii. kalendas aprilis nondum completo post martyrium anno primo: ipsum apud perusium in platea ecclesie fratrum astante sibi plebis clerique ac religiosorum nobilium et magnatum numerosa frequentia;

15 aliis ubertim flentibus per leticia. aliis pluribus laudantibus in sublime: cunctis uero uberrime tripudiantibus et agentibus diem festum; cum sollempnitate non modica et mirabili cereorum ardentium multitudine. et eximio sacrarum uestium apparatu. sanctorum martirum cathalogo statuit ascribendum. Et quoniam dies

20 passionis eiusdem qui fuit octauus dies aprilis inter paschalia festa frequenter occurrit; ipsius festiuitatem ordinauit. iii° kalendas maii. a tocius orbis fidelibus deuote ac sollempniter celebrari. ubi autem per mundum diffusus est apostolice iussionis auditus; mox auditum deuotio. deuocionem uero noua miracula sunt secuta. que inferius in

---

6 studiose] diligenter *TA Taeg*   **7** diligenter] *om. P1 P2 P3 Tr*   **8** sequentem] subsequentem *Taeg*   **9** excrescentiam] excrescere *TA* | ueritatis...famam] ueritatem et famam *TA*   **10** insinuata] nunciata *P1 P3 Tr*   **12** viii...aprilis] IX *Kal.* Aprilis *Taeg* | post] prius *P1 P3 Tr om. TA Taeg* | anno primo] *om. TA* | primo] *add.* post martyrium *Taeg*   **13** ecclesie fratrum] *transp. P3* | fratrum] *add.* predicatorum *TA Taeg* | astante] adstante *TA Taeg* | sibi] *om. TA* add plebi *S exp.* | plebis...**14** clerique] cleri plebisque *P1 P3 Tr* cleris populisque *Taeg*   **14** et] ac *Taeg* numerosa] innumerosa *P1*   **15** ubertim...leticia] *om. TA* | per leticia] pre gaudio *P1 P3 Tr* | pluribus] *add.* deum *TA* | laudantibus...**16** sublime] in sublime laudantibus *P1 P3 Tr add.* tollentibus *Taeg*   **16** uberrime] *om. TA Taeg*   **17** festum] *om. TA* | sollempnitate] solennitate *Taeg* | non modica] magna *TA*   **18** et] *om. Ps* | eximio] et *TA Taeg*   **19** martirum] *add.* catho *P3 exp.* | cathalogo] catalogo *Taeg* | ascribendum] adscribendum *TA Taeg* | Et] *add.* Octaua kalendas aprilis. Pontificatus sui anno decimo; dominice uero incarnationis inchoante anno millesimo cc. quinquagesimo tercio. *TA* | quoniam] *add.* autem *Taeg* | dies...**20** fuit] dies qui fuit passionis *P3*   **20** eiusdem] eius *Taeg om. P1 P2 P3 Tr add.* martyris *TA* fuit] sunt *TA* | octauus dies] octauo kalendas *F* | octauus...aprilis] octaua die

made into his virginal innocence and his abundant merits and miracles so that they might be carefully examined, those which came before and after his triumphal passion. And because he plainly recognized the growing truth of Peter's reputation, and found that was had been communicated to him was less than it actually was, with the concurrence of all cardinals and prelates who then were residing in the Apostolic See, Innocent IV canonized Peter on 25 March 1253, with not even a year having elapsed since his martyrdom. The Pope came to the piazza of the Church of the Friars Preachers in Perugia and – assisted by the clergy, the religious, and the laity, and with a large crowd of nobles and magnates all weeping abundant tears of joy – the Supreme Pontiff ordered that Peter be inserted into the roll of Holy Martyrs. All the others raised lofty praises, by dancing and spending the day in festival, and with an extraordinary multitude of burning candles, and with great splendor of sacred vestments. Because the day of his passion, the 8th day of April, was frequently during the paschal feast, Innocent ordered it celebrated on III Kalends of May with devotion and solemnity by all the faithful. Whence the Apostolic command was circulated throughout the world, soon devotion was stirring, and new miracles followed this devotion, which are recorded below from diverse

---

12 25 ... **13** 1253] This was the date that the Bull was released, Innocent IV actually canonized Peter in Perugia on 9 March 1253.   **21** 8th ... **22** April] This is also incorrect in the manuscripts, but corrected by Taegio. Peter died on the VIII Ides of April, or April 6th.   **23** III ... May] 29 April.

---

mensis aprilis *TA* VIII Idus Aprilis *Taeg* | dies] ydus *S* idus *N W* **21** festiuitatem] festum *Taeg* **22** tocius] totius *Taeg* | fidelibus] *add.* ac *exp. P1* | deuote ac] *om.* *TA* | sollempniter] solenniter *Taeg* | ubi ... **28** integro] *om. Taeg add.* sicut expressius apparet in Apostolicis litteris, universis ecclesiarum Prelatis directis, que sunt infrascripti tenoris. *Taeg* **24** que ... **25** designantur] *om. TA*

25 diuersis mundi partibus designantur. quibus omnibus et ante omnia premittere congruum. quod in translatione martyris apparuit euidenter.

De translatione et inuentione corporis integro.

Beato enim petro martyrum sociato cathalogo. fidelium dignum duxit deuotio sacrum corpus quod ultra annum humili loco sub terra iacuerat: ad altiorem locum decentius transferrendum; ad quod cum fratres apud mediolanum ad prouinciale capitulum conuenissent. ita
5 sanum et integrum ac fine alicuius exalatione fetoris repertum est: ac si eadem die fuisset nouiter tumulatum. fratres igitur super magnum pulpitum iuxta plateam corpus martyris cum magna reuerentia deduxerunt: et ibidem sic sanum et integrum omni populo est ostensum et ab eo suppliciter adoratum.

VII   *de miraculis.*

Porro de miraculis canonizationem eius sequentibus. licet plura et plurima referantur in diuersis prouinciis coruscasse. quedam que fide dignorum attestatione ad nostram notitiam sunt deducta. breuiter

---

26 premittere] promittere *TA* | congruum] congruit *P2 F S Ps N W add.* est *TA* translatione] *add.* eisdem *TA* **28** integro] *om. P1 P3 Tr add.* xlii. *P1 P3 F W add.* xlii capitulum *N* **VI.ii,1** Beato…VI.ii,9 adoratum] Canonizato itaque B. Petro Martyre, multis eum miraculis Dominus dignatus est illustrare. Nam quam plures diversis infirmitatum incommodis laborantes, ad ejus venerabile sepulcrum accedentes, sanitatis remedia B Petri Martyris meritis sunt consecuti. Quapropter fidelium duxit devotio sacrum ipsius Martyris corpus, quod ultra annum sub terra humili loco jacuerat, ad altiorem locum transferre. (Propter quod Fratres ad Capitulum provinciale Mediolanum convenerunt: non enim eodem anno generale Capitulum est celebratum, propter Magistri Ordinis videlicet Fr. Joannis Teutonici decessum, qui post B. Michaelis festum obiit, in quo secundum Ordinis Constitutiones celebrari non debet) levatum est sacrum corpus: quod ita sanum et integrum repertum est, acsi in eadem die sepultum fuisset. Fratres autem presente D. Mediolanensi Archiepiscopo Fr. Leone de Perego, Mediolanensi Patricio, Ordinis Minorum, viro integerrimo et omnia ordinante, Sancti Martyris corpus super magnum pulpitum, juxta plateam ecclesie, magna cum reverentia deduxerunt, et ibidem sic sanum et integrum omni populo est ostensum, et ab eo suppliciter

regions, of which and before all it is fitting to retell what happened at the martyr's translation.

On finding of his incorrupt body and its translation VI.ii

The addition of blessed Peter to the Catalog of martyrs led the devotion of the faithful to transfer the holy body of the martyr, which had lain for a whole year under humble earth, to a more honored place. On this account when the brethren convened for the Provincial Chapter in Milan, [his body was disinterred] and it was discovered to be whole and incorrupt, as if it was newly entombed. Therefore the friars placed the body upon the great pulpit facing the piazza, and with special reverence there presented him, whole and incorrupt, to all the people and by them he was humbly honored.

Of his miracles

Hereafter the narrative will relate the miracles following his canonization, though they are of an exceptional number, shining through different regions. Certain of these have been brought to our knowledge by those who are trustworthy, and we will cover these

---

VI.ii,2 body... 9 honored] Taegio, 7.56; LA, 428-429.

---

adoratum. *Taeg* | enim] itaque *TA Taeg* | petro] *add.* sanctorum *TA* | sociato] annotato *TA* **2** corpus] *add.* eius *TA* | sub... 3 iacuerat] iacuerat sub terra *P1 P3 Tr om. TA* **4** apud] *om. P1 N* **5** integrum] *om. T* | repertum... 6 magnum] *om. P3 add.* rep | est] *om. Ps* **6** si] *add.* in *Taeg* **7** corpus] *add.* eiusdem *T* | cum magna] *transp. T* **8** deduxerunt] add etiam *exp. P1 add.* presente episcopo et cleri ac plebis multitudine copiosa: *T* **10** de miraculis] *om. S W* add xliii. *P1 P3 add.* post eius canonizationem. xliii. *F N add.* capitulum *N* **VII.i,1** eius... 7 refulserunt] *om. T add.* ac etiam translationem eius sequentibus: plurima scripta habetur in libello de gestis ac passione eiusdem. Fidelium atestatione comparata. Que nos ideo in presenti opere scribere pretermisimus studio breuitatis. Quidam uero in sequentibus sub compendio duximus annotanda. *T* **3** dignorum] *add.* narratis *Tr* cancell. | attestatione... notitiam] relatione ad nostram memoriam *P1 P3 Tr* ad... notitiam] ad nostra notitia *P2* | notitiam] *om. add. sup. F*

perstringenda prouidimus: illum ordinem narrationis serie
5 prosequentes ut apropinquis locis ad remota miraculorum narratio
deducatur. Quibus addi potuerunt que postea euenerunt: uel in aliis
remotis prouinciis refulserunt.

de lusore taxilorum a demonibus arrepto et curato.

Nempe preter ea que superius dicta sunt. ad tumbam beati petri
signorum splendor radiis suis refulgere non desinit; ex quibus illud
famosum pretermittendum non est: multa admiratione refertum. Uir
enim quidam nomine roba de meda. cum usque ad uestes in ludo
5 taxillorum omnia perdidisset; domum in sero rediens. cum lucerna
accensa lectum suum adiret. uidens se tam pannis uilibus inuolutum.
et se tot amississe considerans: pre nimia desperatione demones
inuocare cepit. ac eisdem se ore nephario commendare. Statimque tres
demones affuerunt. qui lucernam accensam in solarium proicientes.
10 ipsum per collum arreptum tam fortiter astrinxerunt. ut nullatenus
loqui posset. Quem cum plurimum agitarent. qui erant in domo
inferiori. ad eum ascendentes dixerunt. Quid est quod agis o roba.
Quibus demones responderunt. Ite in pace uestra: et lectos uestros
intrate. Illi autem predicti uiri uocem esse credentes: protinus
15 redierunt. Quibus redeuntibus: cepit multo fortius a demonibus
agitari. Quod illi cognoscentes. sacerdotem protinus aduocauerunt.
Qui cum per beatum petrum demones adiurasset: duo protinus
exierunt. Sequenti autem die ad sepulcrum sancti petri deductus est.
ad quem frater Guillelmus uercellensis accedens; dum demonem

---

4 ordinem narrationis] *transp. P1* | serie] *om. P1 P3 Tr*   **6** que…euenerunt] *om. P3*
7 remotis…refulserunt] prouinciis refulserunt remotis *P1 P3 Tr*   **8** et curato] *om. P1*
P3 Tr N | curato] *add.* xliiii. *P1 P3 F W add.* xliiii *N*   **VII.ii,1** Nempe…VII.ii,3
refertum] *om. TA Taeg* | dicta] scripta *P1 P3 Tr* | tumbam] tubam *Ps*   **4** roba] raba
P1 P3 Tr   **5** perdidisset] perdidisse *P3*   **6** pannis uilibus] transp *P1 Tr Taeg*
8 eisdem se] *transp. Taeg* | nephario] nefando *Taeg* | commendare] committere
Taeg   **9** affuerunt] adfuerunt *Taeg* | accensam] ardentem *P1 P3 Tr om. Taeg*
solarium] solario *Taeg*   **10** astrinxerunt] adstrinxerunt *Taeg*   **11** erant] *om. Taeg*
erant…domo] in domo erant *P3* | domo…12 inferiori] *transp. Taeg*   **12** inferiori]
add. erant *Taeg* | est] *add.* hoc *P1 P3 om. S add.* enim *S exp.* | roba] raba *P1 P3 Tr*
13 demones] *add.* dicentes *P1* | responderunt] *add.* dicentes *P3 Tr* | uestra] *om. P1*

briefly, following their narrative order from the nearest places until we are led to the retelling of the most remote miracles, to which are able to be added those which happened later, or which are reflected back from other remote places.

Of a dice-playing gambler seized by demons and cured VII.ii

Of course beyond those which were detailed above, the splendor of His rays did not cease to shine at the tomb of Blessed Peter, among which that famous one will not be overlooked, filled with so much wonder. There was a man named Roba da Meda, who had lost everything but the clothes on his back wagering on dice playing. Going back to his house at a late hour, he approached his bed with a lit lamp. Seeing himself clothed in such mean attire he considered himself completely lost. After a little while he began to call upon demons in an excess of desperation, and started to commit himself to them with horrible language. Immediately three demons appeared who, throwing the lit lamp towards the roof, seized him so strongly by the neck that he was completely unable to speak. By this they agitated a great many people who were there in the lower floors of the house, and they came up to him saying, "What is this, o Roba what have you done?" To these the demons responded, "Go in peace and get back in your beds." Believing this to be Roba's voice, they immediately went downstairs. When these people had left, the demons began to shake him with increased force. Realizing at last what was happening, the people downstairs immediately called a priest. He adjured the demons in the name of Blessed Peter Martyr, and two of them immediately fled. The following day he was taken to the tomb of Blessed Peter Martyr. When Friar Guglielmo of Vercelli

----

VII.ii,4 There ... 29 penance] Taegio, 14.112.

P2 P3 Tr   **14** credentes] *corr.* credentibus *P3*   **15** redeuntibus] recedentibus *Taeg* multo fortius] *om. Taeg* | demonibus] *add.* multo fortius *Taeg*   **16** aduocauerunt] uocauerunt *Taeg*   **17** petrum] *add.* Mart. *Taeg*   **18** ad] *add.* B. Petri Mart. *Taeg* sancti petri] *om. Taeg* | deductus] ductus *Taeg*   **19** Guillelmus uercellensis] Wilhelmus de Vercellis *Taeg*

20 increpare cepisset: eum quem nunquam uiderat ex nomine uocans ait
frater Guillelme per te nunquam exibo: quia hic noster est et opera
nostra facit. Quem cum interrogasset quo nomine uocaretur. ait
uocor belsephas. Cum uero per beatum petrum adiuratus fuisset:
infirmum in terram proiciens mox exiuit. Et ille perfecte sanus
25 remanens. penitentiam salutarem accepit.

de heretico et fure correpto

Uir quidam nomine obisso credens hereticorum. cum occasione
cuiusdam heretice consanguine sue. ad ecclesiam fratrum uenisset et
ad tumbam sancti petri pergens. duos ibi denarios conspexisset: ipsos
denarios accipiens dixit. bonum est ut istos bibamus. statimque totus
5 cepit tremere: nec de loco eodem aliquatenus potuit se mouere. qui
territus. predictos denarios in loco suo mox restituit. et inde
abscedens. attendens beati petri uirtutem: heresim deseruit. et ad
fidem catholicam se conuertit.

de curatione mulieris demoniace.

Mulier quedam nomine eufemia de loco cortinago mediolanensis
dyocesis. vii. annis a demonibus est uexata. Sed cum ad sepulcrum
sancti petri ducta fuisset; demones eam amplius uexare ceperunt: et
per os eius audientibus cunctis clamare. mariola mariola. petrine.
5 petrine. tunc demones exeuntes. eam quasi mortuam dimiserunt. sed

---

21 Guillelme] Wilhelme *Taeg* | per] pro *Taeg* **22** facit] fecit *F S Ps N W* | ait…23
uocor] respondit *Taeg* **23** belsephas] Belcephas *Taeg* | petrum] *add.* Mart. *Taeg*
24 Et ille] Ipse autem *Taeg* | sanus…25 remanens] *om. Taeg* **25** remanens]
permanens *P1 P3 Tr add.* sanatus de commissis *Taeg* | penitentiam…accepit] *om.*
S | accepit] penitentiam suscepit *Taeg* **26** de…VII.iv,8 infestabant] *F Ps N W and*
Nv invert these two stories. | et] *om. F* | correpto] corrupto *P1 P2 corr. al. man. sup.*
correpto *add.* xlv. *P1 P3 add.* xlvi *F add.* xlvi capitulum *N* **VII.iii,1** quidam]
quidem *P3* | nomine obisso] Obizo nomine *Taeg* | occasione] actione *S corr. al.*
man. sin. occasione **2** fratrum] *om. P1 P3 Tr* **3** tumbam sancti] ecclesiam Fratrum
Mediolani et ad tumbam Beati *Taeg* | duos ibi] *transp. P3* | ibi] ui *P2 exp. add. al.*
man. sup. ibi | conspexisset…4 denarios] *om. Ps N eyeskip add. al. man. subscr. S*
4 denarios] *om. Taeg* | est] *om. P3* | istos] *add. al. man. dex.* per *N* **5** cepit

began to rebuke the demon, a person whom no one saw called his name saying, "Friar Guglielmo, I shall never leave on your account, because this one is ours and he does our work." When asked by what name he was known, he answered "I am called Belcephas." Yet when he was adjured in the name of Blessed Peter Martyr the sick man was thrown to the ground and suddenly the demon came out of him. He received perfect health and a salutary penance.

Of the correction of a heretic and thief VII.iii

A man named Obizo – a heretic – had occasion to visit the tomb of Saint Peter in Milan with one of his female heretical relatives, and there observed two denarii. Grabbing them he said, "Good! With these we can get a drink." Immediately he began to shake and for a while he was unable to move. Thus terrified, he returned the money to its place and departed. Paying heed to the power of Blessed Peter, he abandoned his heresy and converted to the Catholic faith.

On the cure of a female demoniac VII.iv

A woman named Eufemia di Ortinago in the diocese of Milan had been afflicted by demons for seven years. When she was led to the sepulcher of Blessed Peter the demons began to trouble her even more and all heard her shouting, "Mariola, Mariola, Petrine, Petrine." Then the demons fled out of her but left her like one who had died. After a

---

VII.iii,1 A…VII.iii,7 faith] Taegio, 8.59; LA, 434. **VII.iv,1** A…VII.iv,8 celebrated] Taegio, 14.112; LA, 433.

---

tremere] *transp. Taeg* | eodem] illo *P1* eo *P3 Tr* | potuit… mouere] se mouere potuit *Taeg* | qui] quia *S* **6** mox] *om. Taeg* **9** demoniace] *add.* xlvi. *P1 P3 add.* xlv *F W add.* xlv capitulum *N* **VII.iv,1** nomine eufemia] *transp. Taeg* | eufemia] Euphemia *Taeg* | cortinago] cortirugo *P1 P3* **2** vii annis] annis septem *Taeg* | est uexata] *transp. Taeg* | ad] *add.* B. Petri *Taeg* **3** sancti] beati *P1 Tr* | sancti petri] *om. Taeg* | ducta] deducta *Taeg* | eam] *om. Ps* | eam amplius] *transp. P1 P3 Tr* eam *add. al. man. sup. P3* **4** audientibus cunctis] *transp. Taeg* | petrine… 5 petrine] patrine patrine *P3* **5** sed] et *P1*

post modicum plene sanata surrexit. asserebat autem quod diebus dominicis et festiuis. et precipue quando missa celebrabatur: eam demones amplius infestabant.

de restrictione indesinentis fluxus sanguinis.

Uir quidam de canapitio de uilla mazari. nomine rufinus. grauiter infirmatus; nam uena fracta in interioribus partibus exterius indesinenter sanguinem emittebat: ita quod nullius medicine uel medici sibi suffragabatur remedium. sanguine per. ui. dies et noctes
5 continue affluentius effluente: beatum petrum deuote in sui auxilium inuocauit. Qui tam subito sanatus est. ut inter effusam orationem et receptam liberationem nullum pene afffuerit interuallum. Cum autem se sopori dedisset; uidit quemdam fratrem in habitu ordinis predicatorum. grossum facie atque brunum quem socium beati petri
10 martyrem existimabat. sicut uere forme talis exstiterat: qui ex passione palmas plenas sanguine. quodam unguento suaui offerebat eidem dicens. Sanguis adhuc recens est. ueni igitur ad recentem sanguinem sancti petri. Qui euigilans: sepulcrum sancti petri martyris in gratiarum actionem et laudem statuit uisitare.

---

6 post modicum] postmodum *Taeg* | asserebat] asserebant *Taeg* **7** et festiuis] *om.* *P3* | missa] *om.* *Taeg* | celebrabatur] celebratur *P1 P3* | eam] *add.* plus *P3 exp.* **8** demones amplius] *transp.* *Taeg* | infestabant] uexabant *Taeg* **9** sanguinis] *add.* xlvii. *P1 P3 F W add.* xlvii capitulum *N* **VII.v,1** Uir] fuit *P1 P3 Tr* | Uir…VII.v,1 rufinus] Vir quidam de Campitio, Rufinus nomine *Taeg* | mazari] mazati *F S Ps N W Nv* | rufinus] ruphinus *Ps* | grauiter] grauius *P2 F S Ps W* grauissime *N* **2** infirmatus] infirmabatur *Taeg* | nam] qui *P1 P3 Tr* | fracta…exterius] pectoris fracta *Taeg* **3** indesinenter] indesinanter *P3 exp.* | ita…4 remedium] *om.* *Taeg* **4** sanguine] *add.* autem *P1 exp. add.* et *P3 om.* *Taeg* | ui] uii *P3* **5** continue] continuo *Taeg* | affluentius effluente] fluente vena *Taeg* | effluente] affluente *P1 P3 Tr N* | petrum] *add.* Mart. deuote *Taeg* | deuote] *om.* *P1 P3 Tr* | sui] suum *Taeg* auxilium…6 inuocauit] *transp.* *Taeg* **6** est] *add. al. man. sup.* *S* **7** pene] penitus *Taeg* | afffuerit] fuerit *P1 P3 Tr* interfuerit *N* fuit *Taeg* **8** ordinis] *om.* *Taeg* **9** quem socium] *om.* *P1 P3 Tr* **10** martyrem] *add.* x *P3 exp. add.* Fratrem Dominicum *Taeg* | martyrem existimabat] *transp.* *P3* **11** quodam] cum *Taeg* unguento] *add.* quodam *Taeg* **12** igitur] ergo *Taeg* **13** sancti[1]] beati *P1 P3 Tr*

while she arose healed. And she said that on Sundays and Feast days the demons troubled her the most, especially when the Mass was celebrated.

On the healing of one who had a continual flow of blood VII.v

Rufino da Canapicio of the village of Mazari was terribly sick, for his blood constantly flowed from an injured vein in the lower part of his body, so much that he had been unable to find a remedy from either medicine or physician. For six day and nights the blood continually flowed. When he devoutly invoked the aid of Blessed Peter Martyr, he was immediately healed so quickly that there was no interval at all between the utterance of his prayer and his reception of health. When he surrendered himself to sleep he saw a certain Brother in the habit of the Preachers, with a large face and dark complexion, whom he took to be the companion of Blessed Peter Martyr (since that was how he looked in life) and who bore bloody hands from his passion, the apparition offered him a sweet ointment saying, "The blood is still fresh, therefore come to the fresh blood of Saint Peter." Upon awaking Rufino committed himself to visit the tomb of Blessed Peter Martyr in thanksgiving and praise.

VII.v,1 Rufino … VII.v,15 praise] Taegio, 13.107; LA, 435.

---

petri[1]] *add. al. man. sin.* martyris *P3* | sepulcrum … martyris] beati petri martyris sepulcrum *Tr* | sancti[2]] beati *P1 P3* **14** actionem] *om. Taeg* | laudem] laude *Taeg*

de frequentie accensione candele frequenter extincte.

Quedam comitisse de castro cassino yporiensis dyocesis. cum in beato petro specialem deuotionem haberent. et eius uigiliam ieiunarent; cum ad suam ecclesam ut audirent uesperas accessissent: una earum quamdam candelam in honore beati petri martyris. ante quedam altare beati petri apostoli posuit comburendam. Que cum domum redissent sacerdos auaritia ductus ipsam candelam sufflans eam extinxit: sed mox lumen rediit. et denuo ipsam accendit. Secundo ac tertio eam extinxit. sed lumen ut prius rediit. unde tedio affectus chorum intrauit et ante maius altare aliam candelam inuenit. quam clericus in honore beati petri posuerat. qui eius in uigiliam similiter ieiunabat quam sacerdos bis extinguere uoluit. sed nequiuit. Quod uidens clericus iratus dixit. Dyabole non uides apertum miraculum? quod sanctus petrus non uult ut suam candelam extinguas: Territi igitur et stupentes sacerdos et clericus. castrum ascenderunt: et predictum miraculum omnibus narrauerunt.

Ceterum ad honorem autem martyris. in loco martyrii quedam ecclesia est constructa: in qua iuxta eiusdem ecclesie altare cuidam marliano de birago. duplex gratia est miraculose collata. Nam cum per tres menses nec de lecto potuisset exurgere. nec per se in lecto uertere: uel comode se mouere. cumque per annos. xv. catharorum

---

VII.vi,1 Quedam...**VII.vi,15** narrauerunt] This miracle is omitted in the Gui and material, and Taegio relegates it to a footnote, however Antoninus knows it "Cum quedam Comitissa, devotionem specialem habens ad S. Petrum Mart. in vigilia festi ejus jejunasset, et in die candelam notabilem, ad ecclesiam pergens, ante altare ad honorem B. Petri Mart. accensam posuisset, ut tota consumeretur; recedente Domina, Sacerdos ecclesie, avaritia ductus, illam extinxit. Sed statim divina virtus reaccendit. Extinguit Sacerdos secundo et tertio candelam: sed iterum atque iterum divinitus accenditur. Quod cum idem faceret Sacerdos de alia candela, quam Clericus accenderat ante majus altare, in honorem ejusdem B. Petri Mart. vigiliam cujus jejunaverat; lumen rediit ad candelam etiam ipsam extinctam. Tum Clericus iratus Sacerdoti inquit: Diabole, non vides tu miraculum, quia B. Petrus vult quod candela sua ardeat? Territi igitur ex miraculo aliis gesta intimarunt."

---

15 extincte] *add.* xlviii. *P1 P3 F W add.* xlviii capitulum *N*   **VII.vi,4** quedam] *add.* castd *P3 exp.*   **5** apostoli] *add.* p martyris *P3*   **7** ipsam] *add.* ascendit *P3 corr.*

On the frequent relighting of a candle often extinguished   VII.vi

Several noblewomen of the castle of Cassino, of the diocese of Ivrea, bore a special devotion to Blessed Peter and fasted on his vigil. When they went to his church to hear Vespers, one of them lit a candle in his honor before the altar of Blessed Peter the Apostle. When they had returned home, an avaricious priest, led by greed, blew it out. Yet the flame immediately relit and again began to burn anew. He blew it out a second and third time, but the light again returned again. He returned to the choir upset and found a candle before the high altar which had been placed there by a cleric in honor of Blessed Peter, who was there keeping the vigil and fasting. The priest wanted to extinguish this as well. He tried twice but to no avail. When he saw this the clerk said angrily, "Devil! Do you not see the miracle before your eyes? Blessed Peter does not wish that his candle be put out!" The priest and cleric were terrified and dumbfounded, and they went up to the town and told the miracle to all.

A church was built at the place of his martyrdom to further honor   VII.vii
him. At the altar of that church Marliano d'Albirago obtained a double grace by a miracle. He had not been able to arise from bed for three months, nor to even move himself easily, nor even to turn in bed, and he had also been entangled in the errors of the Cathars for

---

VII.vi,1   Several... VII.vi,15 all] LA, 435. | Cassino] LA has Masino.
VII.vii,1   A...8 faith] Taegio, 13.99.

---

9 chorum intrauit] *transp. Ps*   **10** similiter... **11** ieiunabat] *transp. P1 P3 Tr*   **11** sed] *om. P3*   **12** uides] *add.* non *S exp. add.* nonne *N*   **15** omnibus narrauerunt] *transp. P3* | narrauerunt] *add.* xlix. *P1 P3 S F* xlviii c. *W add.* de curatione corporali et spirituali cuiusdam credentis hereticorum. xlix capitulum *N*   **VII.vii,1** Ceterum] *om. TA Taeg* | autem] *add.* sancti petri *TA om. P2 F S Ps N W Nv* | loco] *add.* sui *P1* | quedam] *add.* sunt *TA*   **2** est constructa] *transp. Taeg* | qua] *add.* iuxta *TA Taeg* | iuxta] *om. P1*   **3** birago] Burgo *Taeg* | gratia] *add.* fuit *TA* | est] *om. P1*   **4** potuisset] potuerit *TA* | potuisset exurgere] surgere potuisset *Taeg* | nec² ... **5** uertere] *om. Taeg*   **5** uertere] conuertere *TA* | uel] nec se *TA Taeg* | mouere] *add.* nec se in lecto uertere *Taeg* | cumque] et *Taeg* | annos xv] quindecim annos *TA Taeg* | catharorum] *add.* hereticorum *TA* | catharorum... **6** fuisset] *transp. Taeg*

fuisset erroribus irretitus; illuc spe salutis portatus. et santitatem consecutus est corporis et mente superno lumine illustratus. conuersus est ad fidei ueritatem.

Non fuit autem inter uaria beneficia collata extraneis: beatus matryr fratrum suorum oblitus. duobus enim fratribus predicatoribus. deuote ad ipsius suffragia recurrentibus: beneficia miraculose salutis impendit. Nam cum unus a quodam uehementi apostemate quod
5   patiebatur in costis. iudicio medicorum non posset absque incisione curari. nec sine periculo mortis incidi. cum esset mediolani pauefactus confugit ad martyris monumentum. Dumque suum discrimen beato martyri commendaret. maiori quam postulare presumeret beneficio eius donatus; protinus enim omni tumore cum toto apostemate
10   recedente: fuit absque periculo et incisione curatus.

Alter uero cum esset ydropicus. et medicinis non posset aliquibus naturalem stomachi restaurare calorem; in conuentu astensi ante altare martyris orans: optinuit tocius corporis sanitatem.

Sicut autem frater fratres: sic adiuuabat innocens innocentes. Nam cum quidam puer quidam de tresano mediolanensis. dyocesis. algisestus nomine. ad eius tumulum fuisset a matre delatus; effusis

---

6 et] *om. TA Taeg* | et...7 est] *om. Taeg* | santitatem...7 corporis] consecutus est corporis sanitatem *P1 P3* consecutus est corporis *Tr* corporis sanitatem sortitus est *Taeg* **7** est] est *exp. P2* | illustratus] illustrata *TA Taeg* **8** ad] *om. P3 add. al. man. sin.* | ueritatem] *add.* l. *P1 P3 F* xlix c. *W add.* de curatione duorum fratrum ordinis predicatorum ex deuota inuocatione sancti petri. l capitulum *N* **VII.viii,1** Non...VII.viii,2 oblitus] *om. Taeg* | beatus] *add.* martyre *P3 exp.* **2** duobus enim] duo *Taeg* | fratribus predicatoribus] Fratres Ordinis Predicatorum *Taeg* **3** recurrentibus] recurrentes *Taeg* | miraculose...4 impendit] miraculos sanitatis sunt consecuti *Taeg* **6** curari] cutari *Taeg* | periculo mortis] *transp. Taeg* mediolani] multum *Taeg* **7** confugit...monumentum] ad Martyris tumulum confugit *Taeg* | Dumque] cumque *F* | suum] *om. P3 add. al. man. dex.* **8** martyri commendaret] committeret Martyri *Taeg* | maiori] prius *Taeg add.* et *Ps* presumeret] *add.* est *Taeg* **9** eius] *om. Taeg* | omni] *add. al. man. sup. P3* | cum toto] et *Taeg* **10** recedente] toto *Taeg* | fuit...curatus] *om. Ps* | curatus] no break here *P2 P3 Tr F S Ps N W Nv* **VII.ix,1** Alter] alius *Taeg* | aliquibus] *add.* se iuuare,

fifteen years. He was carried to the church in the hope of healing, whereupon his body was healed and his mind was illuminated by a supernal light, and he was converted to the true faith.

Amidst the various benefits obtained for outsiders, it should not be thought that the blessed martyr was forgetful of his own brethren. Two brothers of the Order of Preachers, devoutly having recourse to his suffrages, were healed following the benefit of miracles. One brother had a serious ulcer in his side which, by the judgement of the doctors, could not be cured without an incision which would leave him in danger of death. At this news he was extremely terrified, and took refuge at the tomb of the Martyr. When he had confided his crisis to the Blessed Martyr, before he dared to hope, the boon was granted to him. Immediately all tumors and ulcers were cured without danger or incision. VII.viii

The other brother was afflicted with dropsy and medicine was not able to help him, nor could it restore natural warmth to his stomach. In the convent of Asti while praying before the altar of Blessed Peter Martyr, he immediately obtained complete bodily health. VII.ix

Just as he was a brother to his brethren, so also did the innocent one come to the aid of innocents. A certain boy of Terzano in the diocese of Milan named Aligiseto was carried by his mother to the tomb. She VII.x

---

VII.viii,3 Two…11 incision] Taegio, 9.67. **VII.ix,1** The…4 health] Taegio, 9.67. **VII.x,2** A…6 them] Taegio, 13.100.

---

nec *Taeg* **2** stomachi] stomachis *Taeg* | astensi] astans *P1 P3* astens *N W* Astanensi *Tr* **3** altare] *add.* man. inf. *P1 add.* B. Petri *Taeg* | optinuit] obtinuit *Taeg add.* protinus *Taeg* | sanitatem] *add.* li. *P1 P3* l. *W add.* de curatione cuiusdam pueri. li. *F add.* de curatione cuiusdam pueri ad tumulum sancti martyris. li capitulum *N* **VII.x,1** Sicut…VII.x,1 innocentes] *om. Taeg* | Sicut…VII.xii,5 restitutam] *om. Tr* | sic] sicut *P3* ut *exp.* | adiuuabat] adiuuabat *P1 exp.* bat Nam] *add.* qui *P3 exp.* | Nam…2 quidam²] puer quidam *Taeg* **2** tresano] Terzano *Taeg* | mediolanensis dyocesis] *transp. P3* **3** algisestus] alissecus *P1 P3* algisecus *S* algisetus *F W Nv* algisitus *N* | eius] B. Petri *Taeg* | fuisset…delatus] a matre delatus fuisset *Taeg*

precibus ad martyrem ut sciebat. salutem manus et pedis et totius
5 dextri lateris quod amiserat impetrauit.

Alius quoque puer de ualle leuentina. nomine soldaninus. ad
eumdem locum non delatus sed oblatus a matre; qui primo totus
contractus fuerat et gibbosus. postea sanus factus et rectus: pedibus
suis uenit. ductus a matre sicut uouerat et oblatus.

Ad eandem ecclesiam quedam puella nomine sabina de dyocesis
nouariensis. similiter a matre ducta: cum manum haberet ita
contractam. ut per digitorum constrictione palmam sibimet unguibus
perforaret: super martyris sepulcrum appositam extendit et protinus
5 sanitati pristine restitutam.
VIII Post hec autem non sunt omittenda que in diuersis uicinis lombardie
partibus claruerunt. ex quibus ut ordo narrationis ordinare decurreret.
aliqua interferenda prouidimus. rem miram ad exaltationem fidei
proferentes in medium. in omnibus enim elementis sanctum suum
5 dominus mirificare adiecit. dum sanctitatem eius. sine sensu singula
perceperunt. et maxima ueneratione dignum. multa etiam elementa

---

4 et²] ac *Taeg* **5** dextri] dexteri *Taeg* | impetrauit] *add.* lii. *P1 P3 S* li. *W add.* De
curatione cuiusdam pueri contracti ex gibbosi. lii *F add.* De curatione cuiusdam
alterius pueri ad inuocationem eiusdem martyris. lii capitulum *N* **VII.xi,1** quoque]
quidam *Taeg* | soldaninus] saldaninus *P1 P3* **2** eumdem] eundem *P1* **3** fuerat]
om. Taeg | gibbosus] *add.* fuerat *Taeg* | sanus] *add.* et incolumis *Taeg* **4** matre]
add. et *Taeg* | sicut] *add.* Sancto Martyri *Taeg* | oblatus] *add.* liii. *P1 P3* lii. *W add.*
de curatione cuiusdam puella. liii *F add.* de curatione cuiusdam puella habentis
manum   contractam   ad   tumulum   sancti   martyris. liii capitulum *N*
VII.xii,1 eandem] eamdem *Taeg* | quedam puella] *transp. Taeg* | de dyocesis] *om.*
Taeg **2** similiter] *om. Taeg* | ducta] deducta *P3* educta *Ps* **3** constrictione]
destrictione *P1* | palmam] palmas *P1 P3* | sibimet] sibi *Taeg* **4** appositam]
apposita *Taeg* | extendit] *add.* manum *Taeg* | et... **5** restitutam] pristina restitutam
Taeg **5** restitutam] restituta est. liiii. *P1 P3* liiii. *W* de diuersis miraculis per eum in
elementis factis. liiii *F* de diuersis miraculis in omnibus elementis quibus dominus
factum suum mirificat. liiii capitulum *N* **VIII.i,1** Post...**VIII.i,4** medium] *om. TA*
Taeg | non...omittenda] obmittenda non sunt *F S Ps N W Nv* | omittenda] *add.*
hec *P1 P3 Tr* **3** rem] esse *P3* **4** in²...**8** illesum] *om. Taeg* | omnibus] singulis *TA*

directed effusive prayers to the Martyr, as far as she knew how, and he regained health in his hand, his foot, and his whole right side, for he had lost use of them.

Another boy of Valle Leventina named Soldanino had not been brought to the tomb, but rather his mother simply offered prayers on his behalf. He who was completely paralyzed with lumps later became healthy and upright. He traveled on his own feet [to the tomb], led by his mother, who made an offering just as she had vowed.   VII.xi

A girl named Sabina from the diocese of Novara was led to the same church by her mother, for she had a hand so badly constricted that, through the compression of her fingers, her nails had pierced her palm. She placed her hand over the tomb of the Martyr, and drew it back restored to its original condition.   VII.xii

Yet after these things, the miracles that occurred in the various parts of Lombardy are not to be omitted, among which we have taken care to insert other things, so that the narration might proceed in an orderly fashion. For the Lord worked to increase the glory of His saint though all the earthly elements, that they might perceive his sanctity not only through a single bodily sense, and so that worthy of the highest veneration, all of the elements offered testimony with great cries. For fire recognized him, and forgetful of the strength of its   VIII.i

---

VII.xi,1 Another…5 vowed] Taegio, 13.100. **VII.xii,1** A…5 condition] Taegio, 13.100.

---

sanctum…5 sensu] adiecit dominus mirificare sanctum suum *TA*   **5** adiecit] elementies *TA* | sanctitatem] sanctitate *TA*   **6** maxima…7 sunt] imita quodam modo protestata sunt *TA*

magnis clamoribus protestata sunt. cognouit enim ignis. dum uim sue
uirtutis oblitus: iniectum frustum tunice beati petri seruauit illesum.

de panno tunice non combusto.

Quidam enim iuuenis nomine guifredus de ciuitate cumana. dum
pannum habitum de tunica sancti reuerentius custodiret. et quidam
hereticus eidem deridendo diceret. quod si sanctum eum crederet.
panum ipsum in ignem proiiceret: et si non comburi contingeret.
5 absque dubio sanctum crederet. et sue fidei fidem daret: mox super
carbones accensos. pannum sancti petri proiecit: sed ab ipso igne
longius resiliuit. deinde per se super carbones rediens: ipsos accensos
et ardentes penitus extinxit. tunc adhuc dicente incredulo. sic per
omnia pannus tunice mee faceret: positus est super delatos carbones.
10 ex una parte pannus heretici: et ex alia pannus sancti. pannus heretici
mox ut ignis calorem sensit: penitus est combustus. pannus uero
sancti petri in ignem preualuit. et ipsum ignem extinxit: ita quod nec
pilus aliquis de eo combustus fuit. Quod uidens hereticus ad uiam
ueritatis rediit. et miraculum omnibus predicauit.

de liberatione nauis naufragantis.

Cognouit aer et aqua: dum ad inuocationem nominis santi petri
tranquillitate reddita. promptam obedientiam ostenderunt. quedam
namque nauis dum in medio maris pene naufragium pateretur: seua
uentorum et fluctuum inundatione cassata. et omnes qui in naui
5 erant caligo tenebrose noctis opprimeret: diuersi diuersorum

---

VIII.i,7 uim…8 oblitus] Antiphon from the Canticle of the Three Young Men at
Lauds on 3rd Sunday of Lent. Comparison of this event with their preservation
from the fire.

---

7 protestata] protesta *P2* | enim] ei *TA* | uim] inde *S exp. corr. al. man. sin.* uim
9 combusto] *add.* lv. *P1 P3 F add.* lv capitulum *N* liiii. *W* **VIII.ii,1** Quidam]
quidem *P3* | guifredus] Gaufredus *Taeg* **2** tunica] *add.* sancti petri *TA*
reuerentius] reuerecius *T* **3** eidem] eiusdem *Ps* **4** ipsum] *add.* p *P3 exp.* **5** dubio]
add. ipse *TA* **7** rediens] radiens *T add.* pannos *T* **8** per…9 omnia] *om. Ps*
9 mee] *add.* hoc *P1 P3 Tr* | faceret] faciet *F S Ps N W Tr* **10** pannus heretici[1]] *om.*

power, kept unharmed the fragment of the tunic of Blessed Peter that had been thrown into it.

Of the cloth tunic that would not burn   VIII.ii

A certain youth of the city of Como named Gaufredo reverently preserved the cloth tunic of Blessed Peter Martyr. It happened that a heretic made derisive comments to him that, if he believed in the saint, he ought to cast the cloth into the fire. He said that if it was not burned, he would believe in the saint without doubt, and he would convert to his faith. At this, Gaufredus threw the cloth tunic of Saint Peter over the burning coals, but for a long time it did not burn, then he turned it over the fire, and the burning was totally extinguished. Still the heretic remained incredulous, saying "The cloth of my tunic would do likewise." So Gaufredo placed burning coals on part of the heretic's cloth tunic, and over a portion of Peter's tunic. As soon as it felt the heat, the heretic's cloth was entirely consumed. Peter's tunic however prevailed over the fire, and extinguished it entirely, so that not any of its threads were harmed. Seeing this, the heretic returned to the way of truth, and made the miracle known to all.

On the deliverance of a ship from shipwreck   VIII.iii

Air and water recognized him, when they showed ready obedience and turned calm at the invocation of the name of Saint Peter. A ship was in danger of shipwreck in the middle of the sea, having been racked with fierce winds and covered by inundating waves, and all who were on the ship were suffering from a fog as thick as night, so

VIII.ii,1 A…VIII.ii,15 all] Taegio, 4.58; LA, 429.   **VIII.iii,2** A…24 Brethren] Taegio, 15.116; LA, 430.

F | ex²] *add.* parte *S Ps N W Nv* | pannus³] *add.* itaque *TA*   **12** ipsum ignem] *transp. F S Ps N W*   **13** pilus] *add.* ex eo *TA* | aliquis] *add.* est *TA* | de…fuit] combustus fuit de eo *P1 P2 P3 Tr* | fuit] *om. TA*   **15** naufragantis] *add.* lvi. *P1 P3 F* lv. *W add.* lvi capitulum *N*   **VIII.iii,1** Cognouit…VIII.iii,2 ostenderunt] *om. Taeg*   **3** namque] enim *TA om. Taeg* | medio maris] mare medio *Taeg* | pateretur] *add.* et *P1*   **5** caligo] *om. TA* | caligo…noctis] tenebrosa caligo noctis *Taeg*

sanctorum suffragia postulabant. sed cum nullum sue liberationis uiderent indicium. seque periclitari plurimum formidarent: quidam de eis natione ianuensis. facto silentio sic eos alloquitur. uiri fratres. numquid non audisitis? qualiter quidam de ordine predicatorum
10 nomine frater petrus. nuper ob defensionem fidei catholice sit ab hereticis interfectus. multaque per eum dominus signa ostendit: nunc igitur deuote suum patrocinium imploremus: quia spero quod nequaquam a nostra postulatione fraudemur. assentiunt uniuersi: beatum petrum in sui auxilium deuotis precibus inuocantes. quibus
15 sic orantibus; mox antena nauis in qua uelum appenditur. cereis accensis tota plena conspicitur: ita quod omni obscuritate illorum cereorum mirabili fulgore fugata: nox illa tam caliginosa in diem clarissimam comutatur. respicientesque quemdam in habitu fratrum predicatorum. super uelum stantem de quo nulli dubium fuit quin
20 beatus petrus extiterit; statim cessauit uentus. mare quieuit. et facta est tranquillitas magna. cum ergo predicti naute ianuam incolumes aduenissent domum fratrum predicatorum. adierunt. deo et beato petro referentes gratias: eisdem fratribus totius miraculi seriem referentes.

de curatione rupte inguinis per appositionem terre

Terra cognouit dum preter naturalem cursum supernaturalem induit: ut non iam terre nascentia. sed dei mirabilia germinaret. scolaris enim

---

7 uiderent indicium] *transp. P1 P3 Tr* **8** de eis] *om. TA Taeg* | ianuensis] Genuensis *Taeg* | facto silentio] *transp. Taeg* | sic] *om. P1 P3 Tr* | alloquitur] *add.* sic *P1 P3 Tr* **9** numquid…audisitis] *om. TA* | qualiter] *om. TA* quod *Taeg* **10** petrus] *add.* de uerona *TA* | nuper] on. *Taeg* | defensionem] defensione *TA* defensionem…catholice] Catholice fidei defensionem *Taeg* | sit] fuit *TA add.* nuper *Taeg* **12** suum] eius *P1 P3 Tr* | suum…imploremus] suum imploremus auxilium *Taeg* **13** postulatione fraudemur] *transp. Taeg* | fraudemur] fraudemus *TA* **14** deuotis precibus] *om. TA* **15** antena] antenna *Taeg* **16** tota plena] *transp. Taeg om. TA* | ita…17 fugata] ita quod illorum cereorum mirabili fulgore obscuritate omni fugata *Taeg* | illorum…17 mirabili] *om. TA* **17** fulgore] *add.* cereorum *TA* | illa tam] illatam *Taeg* | tam] *om. TA Taeg* **18** clarissimam] clarissimum *TA Taeg* | comutatur] commitatur *TA* commutaretur *Taeg* respicientesque] respicientes quod *P3 add.* uiderunt *TA Taeg* | fratrum] *om. Ps W*

they besought the suffrages of several saints. When it seemed that none was able to effect their deliverance, they feared to test any others. Silence having fallen, a Genoese man spoke to the others and said, "Men! Brothers! Have you not heard how one of the Order of Preachers, named Friar Peter, was recently killed in defense of the Catholic faith by heretics, and that the Lord has worked many wonders through him? Now therefore let us implore his aid with devotion, because I expect that we shall not seek in vain." All present assented, invoking the aid of Blessed Peter with their devout prayers. These having prayed, suddenly lit candles appeared all over the ship's mast, upon which hung the sail, so that by the marvellous brilliance of the candles the utter darkness was driven away, and the gloom of night was changed into the clearest day. Looking back, they saw a man in the habit of the Preachers, standing over the sail; there was no doubt it was Blessed Peter. Immediately the wind quieted, the sea calmed, and the greatest tranquility settled over the scene. When the ship arrived in Genoa unharmed, they went to the house of the Friars Preachers giving thanks to God and to Blessed Peter Martyr, and faithfully recounting the miracle to the Brethren.

On the cure of a ruptured groin though the application of earth   VIII.iv

The earth recognized him as well, when it followed a supernatural path beyond the normal course of things, so that it would no longer generate those things that are born of the earth, but rather the

---

19 predicatorum] *add.* uiderunt *P3* | super...stantem] stantem super uelum *Taeg* dubium fuit] *transp. P1 P3 Tr* 20 petrus] *om. S add. al. man. sin.* | extiterit] *add.* et *P3* | statim] statimque *TA Taeg* | mare quieuit] *transp. TA* | et...21 magna] magnaque tranquillitas facta est *Taeg* 21 cum...24 referentes] *om. TA* | ianuam] Genuam *Taeg* 22 deo] Deoque *Taeg* 23 petro] *add.* Mart. *Taeg* | referentes gratias] *transp. P1 P3 Tr Taeg* | totius] *om. Taeg* 24 referentes] fideliter narrauerunt. *Taeg* 25 de...VIII.iv,10 fuit] *om. Tr* | per...terre] *om. Ps* | appositionem] appositum *P1* | terre] *add.* lvii. *P1 P3 F add.* lvii capitulum *N* lvi. *W* **VIII.iv,1** Terra...VIII.iv,2 germinaret] *om. Taeg* | Terra...VIII.iv,10 fuit] *om. Tr* 2 non] *om. A*

quidam cum de magalona ad montem pessullanum rediret. ex quodam saltu adeo est ruptus in inguine ut dolore nimio uexaretur: et incedere non ualeret; hic aliquando audiens predicari. quod quedam mulier terram sanguine beati petri respersam super cancri corrosione ponens. fuerat liberata: dixit: domine deus de terra illa non habeo. sed qui terre illi meritis beati petri tantam dedisti uirtutem: potes etiam isti dare. accipiens igitur de terra cum signo crucis: et in ueneratione martyris loco supposuit. et statim curatus fuit.

de suscitatione puelle.

De remotis autem prouinciis quis sufficiat ennarare miraculorum frequentiam. que in diuersis mundi partibus coruscare cotidie referuntur: prius preteriret nos tempus: quam copia narrandorum. uerumptamen quedam digna memorie. dignum duximus superioribus annectenda. in prouincia namque francie ciuitate senonis. puella quedam cum sub aqua fluminis in quo ceciderat. per longum temporis spatium latuisset: tandem de flumine mortua est extracta. cuius mortis quatuor erant certitudinis argumenta: uidelicet magnum spatium temporis. rigiditas corporis. frigiditas et nigredo. quam cum ad fratrum predicatorum portassent ecclesiam. et eam nouo martyri deuouissent: statim uite est restituta saluti.

---

3 magalona] Magdalena *Taeg* **4** est ruptus] *transp. Taeg* | ruptus] eruptus *F S Ps W* **6** super] *om. Pı P₃* **8** terre illi] *transp. Pı P₃* | potes...9 dare] et isti dare digneris *Taeg* **9** cum...crucis] *om. TA* | signo crucis] *transp. Taeg* **10** martyris] *add.* sancti petri infirmo *TA add.* B. Petri *Taeg* | supposuit] *add.* superposuit *exp. Pı* | curatus fuit] curatus fuit sanatus est *Taeg* **11** de...puelle] *om. P₂ S Ps N W add.* lviii. *Pı P₃* lvii *W* de miraculis que in diuersis prouinciis et remotis per ipsum facta. lviii *F* **VIII.v,1** De] *om. TA add.* Aqua etiam non solum martiris sanguine intincta sed etiam eiusdem martiris tacta reliquiis: nouo curationis genere suscepit uirtutem conferendi mirabiles sanitates. *TA* | De...VIII.v,5 annectenda] *om. Taeg* | quis] *add.* Sed *TA* | ennarare] *add.* circa hic *TA* **2** coruscare] facta sunt: et *TA* **3** narrandorum] narratorum *A* **5** annectenda] connectenda *F S Ps N W add.* de suscitatione puelle in flumine necati *add.* lix *F add.* de suscitatione puelle in

miracles of God. A scholar was going back from Maguelone to Montpellier when, after making a jump, he experienced a rupture in his groin, so that he shook with exceeding pain and was unable to continue on. Then, remembering a sermon about a woman freed from an aggressive cancer through putting the earth sprinkled by the blood of Blessed Peter Martyr on it, he said, "Lord God, I do not have any of that earth, but You who deigned to give such great power to that earth by the merits of Blessed Peter, You are able to give a similar power to this earth." Therefore taking some earth with the sign of the cross and applied it to the injury in honor of the martyr, and immediately he was healed.

On the resurrection of a girl   VIII.v

Who would be capable of retelling the frequency of miracles from the remote provinces that are reported daily shining forth in various parts of the world? The time would fail us before telling all these things, nevertheless we have decided that it was right to add on to earlier things certain stories worthy of memory. In the French province, in the city of Sens, a girl had lain hidden under the water of the river in which she had fallen for a long space of time, and at last she was pulled forth dead from the river. Four things indicated clearly that she was dead: the great length of time [she had been underwater], the rigidity of her body, its coldness, and its blackness. When she was carried to the church of the Friars Preachers, they devoutly commended her to new Martyr, she was immediately restored to her former life and health.

VIII.iv,4 A...14 healed] Taegio, 5.44; LA, 437; VF, 244. **VIII.v,5** In...13 health] Taegio, 10.73; LA, 432; VF, 242.

---

flumine necate lviii capitulum *N W add.* Et quia in prefato libello plura huiusmodi miracula scripta leguntur: in prefati opere pretermisimius studio breuitatis. *TA* namque] uero *T om.* A Taeg | puella] *om. A* **6** sub] in *Taeg* | quo] quam *Taeg* **7** mortua] *om. TA* | est extracta] *transp. Taeg* **8** argumenta] *om. Taeg* **9** spatium temporis] *transp. Taeg* **11** est restituta] *transp. Taeg* | saluti] pristine et sanitati *Taeg*

de suscitatione pueri qui mortuus natus est.

In Flandria quoque. non minoris reuerentie miraculum claruit. nam mulier quedam cum iam tres mortuos filios peperisset. et ex hoc a uiro odio haberetur: beati petri auxilium postulauit. cumque quartum quem postmodum peperit similiter mortuum repeperisset: mater
5 filium defunctum accipiens ad rogandum sanctum petrum totam se contulit. deuotis exorans precibus ut ei filium suscitaret. uix autem orationem compleuit: et ecce puer qui mortuus fuerat uiuus apparuit; quem ad baptisma portatum cum diffiniuissent eum uocare ioannem. sacerdos dum ioannes dicere debuit. nesciens dixit petrus. unde hoc
10 nomen deinceps pro beati petri deuotionem retinuit.

De curatione laborantis in extremis.

In prouincia prouincie arnaldus dictus de marast. de alto uillari laborans in extremis: emisit uotum ut potuit. quod monumentum martyris uisitaret. si eius meritis sibi sanitas prestaretur. cumque cuius uoti senserit manifesta suffragia quam uouens uerba complere
5 ualuerit; ac paulo post plenam salutem fuerit consecutus: quod uouerat non sine multa fatigatione persoluit.

---

12 mortuus…est] natus fuerat mortuus. lix *W* | est] *add.* lix. *P1 P3 add.* lx *F* fuerat. lix capitulum *N* **VIII.vi,1** non…nam] *om. TA Taeg* **2** cum iam] *om. TA* mortuos filios] *transp. Taeg* **3** uiro] *add.* suo *Taeg* | petri] *add.* Mart. *Taeg* postulauit] inuocauit *Taeg* **4** repeperisset] peperisset *TA Taeg* **5** defunctum accipiens] *transp. Taeg* **6** ei] eius *Taeg* **7** compleuit] compleuerat *Taeg* | puer] *om. P1 P3 Tr* **8** portatum] deportatum *Taeg* | diffiniuissent] decreuisset *TA* definitum *Taeg* | eum…ioannem] ut Joannes vocaretur *Taeg* | uocare] *add.* ihonm *P3 exp.* **9** debuit nesciens] voluit, Petrus dixit *Taeg* **10** pro] ob *Taeg* | retinuit] *Gui's* Speculum sanctorale *concludes here add.* Multa quidem et alia signa et miracula operatus est dominus meritis beati petri martiris que hic scripta non sunt. sed plura habentur in predicto libello; Et plurima facta sunt et fiunt cotidie: que scripta non sunt et si scribentur singula. non paruo uolumine claudent *A* …clauderentur *T* **11** De…VIII.vii,6 persoluit] *om. Tr* | extremis] *add.* lx. *P1 P3 add.* lxi *F add.* lx capitulum *N W* **VIII.vii,1** dictus] *om. Taeg* **2** ut potuit] *om. P1 P2 P3*

On the raising of a child who was stillborn

Likewise in Flanders there shone a miracle no less worthy of reverence, where a woman had given birth to three stillborn sons. On account of this her husband harbored a hatred for her, so she called upon the aid of Blessed Peter. And when a fourth was also born dead, the mother took the dead child, and abandoned herself to Saint Peter's suffrages, asking him to resuscitate her son, and praying with devout supplications. Hardly had she completed her prayer when behold the boy who had been dead appeared to live. She carried him for baptism where they decided that he be called John, but when the priest should have said "John" he unknowingly said "Peter" by mistake, wherefore he retained that name ever after in honor of Blessed Peter.

On the cure of one in extreme pain

In the province of Provence, Arnaldus de Marast of Viler le Poterie, laboring in extreme pain, let forth a vow that if he was able, he would visit the tomb of the martyr, if by his merits he might be granted health. Before he felt the effect of the vows, he completed the words with difficulty, but a little later complete health followed, and because he promised, he repaid the vow, but not without much exhaustion.

VIII.vi,1 Likewise...VIII.vi,12 Peter] Taegio, 10.73; LA, 430-431; VF, 241.
VIII.vii,1 In...VIII.vii,6 exhaustion] Taegio, 11.88.

---

monumentum] sepulcrum *Taeg* **3** eius] *om. Taeg* | meritis] *add.* sancti Martyris
Taeg | cuius] prius *Taeg* **4** quam] *om. P3 add. al. man. dex.* **5** fuerit] sit *Taeg*
6 fatigatione] *add.* humiliter et devote *Taeg*

de mirabilis curatione cuiusdam horribiliter tumefacti per totum.

De yspania uero illud sufficiat. quod in ciuitate compostellana. anno domini. m. cc. lix. euidentius claruisse narratur. ubi quidam uir affuit nomine benedictus qui tibias inflatas habebat in modum utris; uentrem tumente ad instar pregnantis. faciem pre nimio tumore
5 horribilem: totumque corpus inflatum ita ut monstrum aliquid uidetur. hic cum a quadam muliere uix se super baculum sustentans. elemonsinam peteret. illa respondit. Magis fossa quam cibo aliquo indigeres. Sed meo consilio ad adquiescens; perge ad domum fratrum predicatorum. et peccata tua confitens: beati petri martyris patrocinia
10 inuocare non cesses. Ille autem cum summo diluculo ad domum fratrum uenisset. matyris imploraturus auxilium. et clausum esse hostium repperisset: secus portam se posuit et dormiuit. Et ecce quidam reuerendus in habitu predicatorum eidem apparuit. qui cappa ipsum cooperiens. eum in ecclesia introduxit. et intra ecclesiam se

---

7 de … totum] de…totum De cuiusdam mirabili curatione horribiliter tumefacti. lxi *P3* | per totum] *om. P1 P3 Tr* | totum] *add.* lxi. *P1 add.* lxii *F add.* lxi capitulum *N W* **VIII.viii,1** De … VIII.viii,17 liberato] "Fuit in civitate Compostelle, ubi B. Jacobi Apostoli venerabile corpus requiescit, juvenis quidam Benedictus nomine, qui ad tantam devenit infirmitatem, ut omnino morti propinquus a videntibus crederetur, erant siquidem tibi ejus inflat in modum utrium, venter ejus ut pregnans; facies autem tanti horroris erat, quod sicut monstrum timorem aspicientibus inferret; presertim cum oculi emergentes exire de corpore viderentur, et cum totum corpus inflatum esset quasi fistula, et vix jam posset vel super baculum moveri. Hic igitur tali modo gravatus, e vespere quodam se utcumque sustentans, ad domum cujusdam devoti, qui Fratres radere solebat, venit, et ab uxore illius multis presentibus eleemosynam petivit. Mulier vero pietate et admiratione commota, Magis, inquit, tibi fossa, quam cibus opus esset: nihilominus meo acquiesce consilio, et ad domum FF. Predicatorum perge, ibique peccata tua confitens B. Petrum novum Martyrem devote depreceris: certa enim sum, quod, si bene oraveris, sanitati pristine continuo restitutus eris. Haec autem devota mulier asseruit plena fide, B. Petri Mart. virtutem in se pluries jam experta: infirmus vero accepto pane ac butyro a muliere, quod dixerat se facturum promisit. Illa autem die qua promiserat non implevit: mane vero sequentis diei ad domum Fratrum veniens, cum adhuc ostium exterius clausum esset, secus portam se posuit ac dormivit. Dum autem dormiret, quidam venerandus Frater Predicator eidem in somnis apparuit, cappa cooperuit, et per dexteram

On the wondrous cure of one whose whole body was swollen   VIII.ix

From Spain let one suffice, which is said to have shone out more clearly in the city of Compostela in the year of the Lord 1259. There was a youth named Benedict whose shins were swollen like wineskins, his stomach was like that of a pregnant woman, and his face repulsive thanks to a tumor, and all of his body swollen such that he seemed like a monster. Supporting himself on crutches, he asked a women for alms. She replied, "You need a grave more than any food, but just the same listen to my advice. Go to the house of the Friars Preachers. There confess your sins and devoutly pray to Blessed Peter Martyr without ceasing." When he reached, right at daybreak, the house of the brethren in order to implore the aid of the Martyr, and found the outer door locked, he placed himself at the gate and fell asleep. Behold a venerable Friar Preacher appeared to him, covered him with his cappa and led him into the church. [When he awoke] he found himself inside the church and perfectly healthy. Everyone who had

---

VIII.ix,2 in[1] ... 17 astonishment] Taegio, 12.93; LA, 437-438; VF, 245-246.

---

manum ipsum tenens in ecclesiam introduxit: invenit autem se evigilans ad ecclesie ostium interius, super gradus, perfecte sanum et corde alacrem. Mira res! Inflatus et immobilis, sanus factus et velox, ad dictam feminam statim cucurrit: in vicoque illo, coram eis qui die precedenti pene mortuum viderant, dixit: Ecce quod mihi dixisti adimplevi, vide quid B. Petrus suis meritis circa me operatus est. Mulier vero juvenis tibiam apprehendens, jam quidem perfecte sanatam, sed in tanti miraculi testimonium adhuc lividam, viro suo vicinisque presentibus, qui eum die precedenti infirmum in vico viderant, coram omnibus juxta B. Jacobi ecclesiam exclamavit: Ecce Dei nostri miracula, ecce mirabilia: heri inflatus, sensu, verbo, gressu deficiens, pene mortuus, sine tumore incolumis laudat Deum. Hunc juvenem multi ex Fratribus nostris sanum viderunt, et infirmum similiter plusquam quingenti ex eadem civitate homines." *Taeg* | yspania] *add.* n *P₃ exp.*   **2** claruisse narratur] *transp. P₁*   **6** muliere] *om.* P₂ F S P₅ W | se] *om.* P₂ S P₅ N W | baculum] *add.* se P₂ S P₅ N W *add.* ex P₃ exp.   **7** cibo aliquo] aliquo cibo P₃ aliquo alio P₁ alio aliquo *Tr*   **10** inuocare] *add.* imploraturus S exp.   **13** quidam] quidem P₃   **14** introduxit] *add.* ille autem euigilans P₂ F S P₅ N W Nv *add.* Ille autem euigilans et intra ecclesiam se repperit. *P₃ add. al. man. sup. P₁*

15 reperit et perfecte sanatum inuenitur. Quod omnibus uidentibus
admirationem intulit et stuporem. de homine pene mortuo sic subito
liberato.

De curatione detractorum contra uenerantes festum suum per filum
tinctum sanguine et curatione febris acute.

De theutonia autem duo mirabilia. uel memorabilia memorari
sufficiat: numquam a memoria hominum abolenda. In illa enim
prouincia apud traiectum mulieres quedam uidentes ad ecclesiam
fratrum predicatorum. in honorem sancti petri martyris magnum
5 concursum fieri populorum; dum ipse in platea consisterent et
filarent: astantibus sic dicebant. Ecce isti predicatores: omnem
modum lucrandi nouerunt. Nam ut magnam possint pecuniam
cumulare. et lata edificare palatia: unum nouum martyrem
inuenerunt. Quibus hec et similia dicentibus; ecce subito filum totum
10 sanguine cruentatur: et digiti quibus filum torquebant. sanguine mox
replentur. Quod ille uidentes et admirantes digitos diligenter
abstergunt. ne forte in eis ex incisura aliqua prouenisset. Sed cum
digitos sanos omnino conspicerent, et filum sic sanguinolentum
uiderent: trementes ac penitentes dicere ceperunt: Uere quia pretioso
15 sanguini martyris detraximus: nobis hoc sanguinis prodigium tam
stupendum euenit. Currentes igitur ad domum fratrum; priori omnia
exposuerunt: filum cruentatum sanguine presentantes. Prior autem ad
multorum instantiam sollempni predicatione indicta; quidquid

---

19 acute] *add.* lxii. *P1 P3 W add.* lxiii *F add.* lxii capitulum *N* **VIII.ix,1** De...
VIII.ix,3 apud] In provinica teutonie apud *Taeg* | uel] duoque *P3* et duo *Tr*
3 traiectum] tinitum *P1* tinctum *P3 Tr* | uidentes ad] et *S* uidentes ad *add. al.*
man. sin. **4** sancti] beati *Taeg* **5** concursum] *om. Taeg* | populorum] *add.*
concursum *Taeg* **6** astantibus] adstantibus *Taeg* | omnem...7 nouerunt] omnes
lucrandi modum invenerunt *Taeg* **7** pecuniam...8 cumulare] *transp. P3 Tr*
8 unum] *om. Taeg* | nouum] *add.* nunc *Taeg* | martyrem...9 inuenerunt] *transp.*
Taeg **10** cruentatur] *add.* est *P3* | digiti] *add. al. man. marg. sin.* ibus *P1* *add.*
quibus *Taeg* | torquebant] torquebatur *Taeg* **12** in] hoc *P1 P3 Tr* | ex] *add. al.*
man. sin. P3 | aliqua] *om. Taeg* | cum] dum *Taeg* **13** sanos omnino] *transp. P1 P3*
Tr Taeg **14** pretioso] pretiosi *Taeg* **15** sanguini martyris] *transp. Taeg* | detraximus]

seen him before on the point of death and now suddenly healed, were filled with wonder and astonishment.

On the cure of those who denigrated those devoted to Peter on his feast, VIII.x
and saw their threads tinged with blood, and another cured of serious
fever

From Germany there were two miracles whose memorable nature it suffices to recall, that they might never be abolished from the memory of men. In that province in the town of Utrecht certain women, when they were milling about in the square and spinning wool, saw the church of the Friars Preachers filled with a great multitude, and standing by said, "Behold these Preachers know every way to make money. Now they discover a new martyr so that they are able to accumulate riches and build spacious palaces." Having said this among other things, suddenly the whole of the yarn became stained with blood, and their fingers which had been spinning the thread were covered in blood as well. Seeing this and marveling they began to wash off their fingers diligently, in case the blood came from a cut. When they saw that their fingers themselves were completely unhurt, and saw the blood-soaked yarn, they began to say tremblingly and penitently, "Truly, because we have spoken ill of the precious blood of the Martyr, this stupendous prodigy of blood has happened." Running to the house of the brethren they told everything to the prior, presenting their blood-stained yarns. And the prior, encouraged by many, decreed a solemn sermon would be held: he retold

---

VIII.x,3 In...VIII.xi,2 talk] Taegio, 8.60; LA, 431

---

detrahimus *P1 P3 Tr* | sanguinis prodigium] *transp. Taeg* **16** igitur] *om. P3*
priori omnia] *transp. Taeg* **17** cruentatum] *om. S space left for word* | cruentatum
sanguine] *transp. Taeg* | ad...18 sollempni] ad mulierem instantiam et multorum
sollempni *P1 P2 P3 Tr*

20 predictis mulieribus acciderat. coram omnibus retulit. et filum cunctis cruentatum ostendit.

Uerum quidam magister artis grammatice in eadem predicatione consistens. factum ipsum cepit malitiose peruertere: et astantibus dicere. Uidete modo qualiter isti fratres: simplicium corda decipiunt. Nam cum aliquibus mulierculis de suis familiaribus condixerunt. ut

5 filum ipsum in aliquo sanguine tingerent: et sic miraculose accidisse narrarent. Dum hoc ille diceret. plagam protinus diuine ultionis excepit; et in ipsum ualidissimarum febrium impetus irruens. multis conspicientibus sic uexauit: ut de predicatione ipsa inter manus amicorum in domum propriam deferretur. Sed cum uehementer

10 febris excresceret. et ille mortem uicinam timeret; predictum priorem accersiri fecit: et reatum suum confitens: deo et beato petro coram dicto priore uotum uouit. quod si eius meritis sanitatem reciperet. eum semper in speciali deuotione haberet. et de cetero linguam ad talia non laxaret. mira res. mox ut predictum uotum protulit protulit:

15 integram sanitatem recepit.

de leui impulsione nauis ornate lapidibus

Quadam etiam uice cum supprior predicti loci quosdam pulcherrimos lapides et magnos in quadam naui duceret: et nauis ex improuiso cuidam littori sic inheseret. ut nullatenus posset moueri.

---

19 mulieribus acciderat] *transp. Taeg* | et…cunctis] filumque *Taeg* **20** ostendit] *no break P1 P2 P3 F S Ps N Tr W Nv* **VIII.x,1** quidam] quidem *P3* | magister] *om. Taeg* | grammatice] *add.* magister *Taeg* | predicatione…2 consistens] *transp. Taeg* **2** ipsum] illud *Taeg* | et astantibus] adstantibusque *Taeg* **3** modo] quomodo et *Taeg* | modo qualiter] quomodo *P1 P3 Tr* **4** cum] *om. P2* | cum aliquibus] quibusdam *P1 P3 Tr* | condixerunt] dixerunt *P1 P3 Tr* dicebant *P2* **5** sanguine tingerent] *transp. Taeg* | sic] *add.* quod *Taeg* | accidisse] accidisset *Taeg* **7** irruens] irruent *P3* **8** manus…9 amicorum] *transp. Taeg* **9** in] ad *P2* | propriam deferretur] *transp. Taeg* | deferretur] referretur *P3 Tr* | cum] dum *Taeg* **10** et… timeret] *om. Taeg* | mortem uicinam] *transp. P1 P3 Tr* **11** reatum suum] *transp. P1 P2 P3 Tr* **13** semper] *om. Taeg* **14** res] *add.* et *P1 exp.* | predictum] *om. P1 P3 Tr* protulit[1]] emisit *Taeg* **15** integram sanitatem] *transp. Taeg* **16** de…VIII.xi,10 remearunt] *om. Tr* | lapidibus] *add.* lxiii. *P1 P3 W add.* lxiiii *F add.* lxiii capitulum

whatever had happened to the aforementioned women before everyone, and showed to all the blood-stained yarn.

Later a certain German grammar master in the province, having attended the same sermon, began to make wicked talk about the goings on, and standing began to say, "See how these brothers deceive the hearts of the simple! For instance, when some silly women agreed with their friends that they should stain their yarns with blood, and so tell a tale of how it happened miraculously." As soon as he said this, he received the scourge of divine wrath, and he was swiftly afflicted with the strongest of fevers, so that he had to be carried to his own house in the hands of his friends. But when the fever grew more vehement, and he feared himself near death, he called the prior to come to him and, confessing his sin, in the presence of the prior he swore a vow to God and Blessed Peter, that if he might receive the benefit of health, he would hold him in special reverence, and that he would not allow his tongue to relax in narrating the details of the miracle. Wonderful thing! As soon as the vow was uttered, he received his health entirely back.

VIII.xi

On the easy dislodging of a stuck ship carrying ornate stones

VIII.xi
i

One time the subprior of the same convent had been transporting large beautiful stones on a certain ship. Without warning the ship struck a sandy bank, and was unable to be moved at all. The sailors

---

VIII.xi,1 master in] For Solemn Preaching, See M. Michèle Mulchahey, *"First the Bow Is Bent in Study. . ."*: *Dominican Education Before 1350*, (Toronto: Pontifical Institute of Medieval Studies, 1998), 183–184. | Later...VIII.xi,16 back] Taegio, 8.60; LA, 431-432. **VIII.xii,1** One...VIII.xii,11 cheerful] Taegio, 15.116; LA, 432.

N **VIII.xi,1** Quadam...VIII.xi,10 remearunt] *om. Tr* | etiam] *om. Taeg* | uice] *add.* contigit *exp. P1* | predicti loci] conventus Trajectensis in Teutonia *Taeg* **2** quadam naui] *transp. Taeg* | et nauis] *om. Taeg* **3** inheseret] hereret *P1 P3* heseret *P2* inhesisset *F* inheserit *P3 N W corr. al man. dex.* inherserit *S* | posset moueri] *transp. Taeg*

Descendentes uero naute omnes ipsam unanimiter impellentes.
5　nullatenus mouere possent; et nauem se amisisse putarent: subprior
omnibus alis amotis. manum ad nauem apposuit. et leuiter ipsam
impellens dixit. In nomine sancti petri martyris in cuius honorem
lapides deferimus: uade. Statimque nauis uelocissime mota de littore:
integra et illesa recessit; super quam naute ascendentes: sani omnes et
10　hylares ad propria remearunt.

de curatione monialis constantiensis. dyocesis.

In eadem prouincia quedam sanctimonialis in claustro octobar.
ordinis sancti sixti. dyocesis. costanciensis existens; per annum et
amplius. grauem guttam in genu perpessa est: ita quod nullo remedio
poterat liberari. Et quia sepulcrum beati petri uisitare corporaliter non
5　poterat. quia nec licebat propter obedientiam. nec ualebat propter
infirmitatem; audiens quod in xiiii diebus de loco illo mediolanum.
possit adiri: cogitauit saltem predictum sepulcrum mentali gressu ac
deuotione sedula uisitare: pro qualibet dieta cotidie. centum.
pater-noster proponens dicere in honorem beati petri. Mirum in
10　modum cum tales dietas cepisset facere. successiue. semper et
paulatim cepit melius se habere. At ubi ultimam dietam perfecit et ad
tumbam mentali gressu peruenit; flexis genibus. ac si presentialiter
coram tumba staret: psalterium cum deuotione maxima totum legit.
quo completo ab illa infirmitate adeo liberatam se sensit: ut iam inde

---

4 Descendentes] Discedentes *Taeg* | uero] autem *P1* quia *P3* | omnes] quod *Taeg*
impellentes] *add.* cum *P1 exp.* 　**5** subprior] subito prior *P3* 　**6** alis] *om. Taeg*
ipsam] eam *Taeg* 　**7** honorem] honore *Taeg* 　**8** lapides] *add.* istos *Taeg* | Statimque]
Statim *Taeg* 　**9** super] supra *Taeg* | sani] salvi *Taeg* | omnes] *om. Taeg*
10 remearunt] redierunt *Taeg* 　**11** constantiensis] *om. Ps* | dyocesis] *om. Tr add.*
lxiiii. *P1 P3 add.* lxv *F add.* lxiiii capitulum *N W* 　**VIII.xii,1** prouincia] *add.*
Teutoni *Taeg* | quedam sanctimonialis] *transp. Taeg* | octobar] ocobat *S F W Nv*
othenbach *N* Eccebach *Taeg* 　**4** poterat liberari] *transp. Taeg* | corporaliter... 5
poterat] non poterat corporaliter *P1 P2 P3 Tr* 　**5** nec[1]] non *Taeg* 　**6** xiiii]
quatuordecim *P3 Tr Taeg* | de] a *Taeg* 　**7** possit adiri] *transp. Taeg* | predictum
sepulcrum] *transp. Taeg* 　**8** cotidie] *om. Taeg* 　**9** pater-noster] *add.* quotidie *Taeg*
proponens dicere] *transp. Taeg* | beati] sancti *Taeg* | petri] *add.* Mart. *Taeg*

disembarked and, even when pushing as one, were unable to dislodge it, and they considered the ship lost. The subprior had placed his hand to the ship after all the others, and lightly pushing her he said, "In the name of Saint Peter Martyr, in whose honor we are transporting these stones, move!" Immediately the ship quickly moved, and pushed away from the bank whole and undamaged. The sailors reentered the ship and they all returned home unharmed and cheerful.

On the cure of a nun of the diocese of Konstanz   VIII.xi ii

In the same province [of Germany] there was a certain cloistered nun of Ottenbach, in the diocese of Konstanz, in the order of San Sisto, who had endured for a year and more painful gout in her knee. No remedy was of any avail. She herself was unable to visit the sepulcher of Blessed Peter (because she was not allowed on account of religious obedience nor was she capable on account of sickness), but hearing that one could make a journey to visit that place in Milan in fourteen days, she decided to visit the tomb by mental steps and attentive devotion, proposing for her regimen to recite one hundred Our Fathers each day in honor of Blessed Peter. In a marvelous way, when she had begun, little by little she began to have better health, and was always improving. When she had reached the last day of her regimen, she arrived at the tomb by mental progress, and she knelt down as if she was really before the tomb, and she read her whole psalter with the greatest devotion: this done, she felt herself so free from all

---

VIII.xiii,1 In … VIII.xiii,18 healed] Taegio, 9.72; LA, 434-435.   **2** San Sisto] The 13th-century name for the cloistered Dominican nuns.

---

10 cepisset facere] *transp. Taeg*   **11** cepit] cepisset *P1* | melius se] *transp. Tr* | se] *om. Taeg* | habere] *add.* cepit *Taeg* | perfecit] fecit *Taeg* | et] *om. Taeg*   **12** gressu] progressu *Taeg* | presentialiter] *om. Taeg*   **13** staret] foret *Taeg* | cum … maxima] maxima cum deuotione *Taeg* | legit] perlegit *P3 Tr*   **14** completo] expleto *F S Ps N W Taeg* | illa] omni *Taeg* | liberatam] *om. P3* | sensit] *add.* ita *Taeg* | inde] *om. Taeg*

15   modicum quid sentiret. Rediens uero eo modo quo iuerat; antequam omnes dietas expleuisset: tota penitus est sanata.

De liberatione cuiusdam fratris ex deuotione festi.

Huic miraculo non immerito annectendum uidetur: quod in fratre iohanne polono resplenduit. Cum enim apud bononiam laboraret quartana et in festo sancti petri sermonem facere deberet ad clerum; accessionem eadem nocte iuxta cursum febris exspectans: uehementer
5   extimuit. ne in iniuncto sibi sermone deficeret. Conuersus igitur ad sancti petri suffragia: ad altare ipsius cum deuotione accessit: orans ut eius meritis iuuaretur. cuius debebat gloriam predicare. Sicque factum est: quod in illa nocte penitus cessauit. et postmodum eum numquam inuasit.

De ungaria uero illud memorari sufficiat: quod in quodam ungaro nomine henrico apertius euenisse compertum est. nam crebrescentibus miraculis multorum relatione longe lateque diffusis; cum dictus hungarus longa perigrinatione mediolanum de peste
5   ciuitate hungarie peruenisset. quoniam sic affligebatur febribus ut nichil penitus febre durante uideret: emisso uoto quod ad locum pergeret. in quo corpus martyris requiescit. si per eum dominus

---

15 iuerat] fuerat *P1*   **16** expleuisset] exolvisset *Taeg* | tota] *om. Taeg* | est sanata] *transp. Taeg*   **17** festi] *add.* lxv. *P1 P3 W add.* lxvi *F add.* lxv capitulum *N* **VIII.xiii,1** Huic…VIII.xiii,2 resplenduit] *om. Taeg* | annectendum uidetur] adiciendum est *P1 P3 Tr*   **2** Cum…3 quartana] In conventu Bononiensi Fr. Joannes Polonus quartana laborabat. *Taeg*   **3** et] Cum autem *Taeg* | sancti] beati *Taeg* petri] *add.* Mart *Taeg* | facere…clerum] ad clerum facere deberet *Taeg* | clerum] *add.* et *P1*   **4** exspectans] exspectaret *Taeg*   **5** igitur] itaque *Taeg*   **6** petri] *add.* Mart. *Taeg* | ipsius] *add.* magna *Taeg*   **8** quod in] ut febris *Taeg* | penitus] *add.* breuis *S exp.* | eum] *add.* non cessant *P3 exp.*   **9** inuasit] euasit *corr. al. man. sup.* inuasit *P1 add.* de miraculis hybernie per aquam lauacri reliquiarum *S add.* lxvi. *P1 W add.* de quodam ungaro similiter per ipsum a febre grauissima liberato. lxvii *F add.* de miraculis factus hybernie per accessum reliquiarum. lxvi *N*   **VIII.xiv,1** De… VIII.xiv,2 nam] uir quidam, Henricus nomine, Hungarus natione fuit, qui cum *Taeg*

infirmity, that she felt only a little pain. She returned the way she had gone, and before she had performed all her exercises, she was thoroughly healed.

On the deliverance of a certain brother on account of his devotion to
Peter's feast

VIII.xi

v

It seems fitting to append to this miracle one which shone brightly for Brother John of Poland, when he labored under a quartan fever in the convent of Bologna on the day he that was supposed to preach a sermon on the feast of Blessed Peter Martyr to the clerics. As he awaited the fever's crisis in the course of the night, he was afraid that he might be too weak to fulfill his duty of preaching. Therefore turning to the suffrages of Saint Peter Martyr, he approached his altar with great devotion, praying that he might be assisted by the saint's merits, whose glory he was about to preach. So it happened that the fever ceased that very night and after that never attacked him again.

From Hungary let this suffice to be remembered, that there was a man named Henry from the nation of Hungary who, when the stories of the many miracles of the martyr became diffused, came on a long pilgrimage to Milan from the Hungarian city of Pest. His fevers were so severe that they seemed nothing other than an extremely painful inner paroxysm, and he let forth an oath that he would go to the place in which the body of the holy martyr lay, if through him the

VIII.xv

VIII.xiv,1 shone…10 again] Taegio, 9.67; LA, 432-433; VF, 248. **VIII.xv,1** From] Similar to Gui: "Terra cognouit dum preter naturalem cursum: super naturalem induit ut iam Aqua etiam non solum martiris sanguine intincta. sed etiam eiusdem martiris tacta reliquiis: nouo curationis genere suscepit uirtutem conferendi mirabiles sanitates. Sed quis sufficiat ennarare circa hic miraculorum frequentiam que in diuersis mundi partibus facta sunt: et cotidie referuntur: prius perteret nos tempus: quam copia narratorum." | there…9 vowed] Taegio, 12.89.

---

3 miraculis] *add.* Martyris *Taeg* | multorum] multorumque *Taeg* **4** cum… hungarus] *om. Taeg* | peste] Pessiensi *Taeg* **6** febre] paroxysmo *Taeg* | quod] *add.* iret *Taeg* **7** pergeret] *om. Taeg* | corpus martyris] sancti Martyris corpus *Taeg* eum] *om.* P2 *add.* sibi F S Ps N W | dominus] *add.* sibi P2

concederet beneficium sanitatis. continuo liberatus. quod uouerat adimpleuit.

IX *De miraculis hybernie.*

Ut autem ab ultimis terre finibus. laudes iusti et gloriam finaliter audiamus; et in fine huius opusculi mirabilia que in honorem martyris in hybernia refulserunt: duximus breuiter apponenda. ubi nouo curationis genere. aqua martiris tacta reliquis. uim conferendi

5 mirabiles sanitates non inordinate suscepit. Ignis namque per se in lampadibus exortus: iam pluries eius honorauerat sepulturam. aer ether locum passionis eiusdem perfusione celestis luminis: sepius maxima dignum ueneratione ostenderat. Terra quoque ipsius aspersa cruore: multis uirtutibus martyris preciosum agonem extulerat. Unde

10 reliquum relinqui non debuit elementum: quin ad dei gloriam in laudem martyris elementa precedentia sequeretur.

De curatione tumoris et doloris pedis ac tibie per aquam predictam.

In quadam enim uilla eloriensis dyocesis. eiusdem prouincie. quidam nobilis helyas nomine. ex uehementi tumore pedis ac tibie. sic grauiter dolore intollerabili cruciatus. ut uel quiescere uel ire. uel cibum sumere non ualeret. cum in tali angustia biduo ieiunasset;

VIII.xiv,10 ... IX.i,5 sanitates] Similar to Gui: "Terra cognouit dum preter naturalem cursum: super naturalem induit ut iam Aqua etiam non solum martiris sanguine intincta. sed etiam eiusdem martiris tacta reliquiis: nouo curationis genere suscepit uirtutem conferendi mirabiles sanitates. Sed quis sufficiat ennarare circa hic miraculorum frequentiam que in diuersis mundi partibus facta sunt: et cotidie referuntur: prius perteret nos tempus: quam copia narratorum."

---

8 concederet] *add.* ei *P3* | concederet beneficium] *transp. Taeg* | uouerat] *add.* fideliter et deuote *Taeg* 10 De...hybernie] *om. S add.* lxvii *P1 P3 W add.* per aquam lauari reliquias sancti. *F W add.* lxviii *F add.* de miraculis et ceteris ut supra. lxvii capitulum *N* **IX.i,3** ubi...4 nouo] *om. S add. al. man. dex.* 4 nouo] *add.* g *P3 exp.* 7 ether] etiam *P2 F S Ps N W Nv* | eiusdem] *om. P2* 9 agonem] agone *Ps*

Lord might give the benefit of heath. Without delay he was freed, and he fulfilled that which he had vowed.

On miracles from Ireland

So that we might finally hear from the furthest ends of the earth the praises and glory of the just man we have decided to briefly add to the end of this work the wonders which shone forth for the honor of the martyr in Ireland, where – as a new kind of cure – water touched by the relics of the martyr received the power to confer wondrous healings, and all in accord with nature herself. For the fire springing up of its own accord in lamps had already honored his tomb several times. The airy aether had shown that the place of his passion was worthy of the greatest veneration by an outpouring of heavenly light. The earth also, sprinkled with blood, had exalted the precious agony of the martyr with many mighty works. Wherefore the remaining element should not be left behind, for it followed the previous elements in the praise of the martyr for the glory of God.

On the cure of tumors and pains of feet and legs through the abovementioned water

In a village of the diocese of Limerick there was a nobleman named Elias who was tormented by a terrible tumor in his foot and he found it intolerable. He was unable to rest or to travel or to even take any food. After he had fasted in such agony for two days, for three days he tasted only the water that had been sanctified by contact with the

---

IX.ii,1 In … IX.ii,13 Martyr] Taegio, 14.108.

Unde] *add.* et *Ps* **11** sequeretur] sequerentur *F* **12** et … predictam] *om. P1 P2 Tr add.* lxviii. *P1 W add.* lxix *F add.* lxviii capitulum *N* **IX.ii,1** enim] *om. Taeg* eloriensis dyocesis] oloriensis diocesis *P1 P3 Tr* | eiusdem] prefate *Taeg* **2** nobilis] *om. Taeg* | helyas] Elias *Taeg* | ac] et *P1 P3 Tr* **3** grauiter] *add.* cruciatus *P1 P3 Tr* | cruciatus] *om. P1 P3 Tr add.* est *Taeg* | ut] nichil *P1 P3 Tr* | uel²] nichil *P1 P3 Tr* | uel³ … 4 ualeret] aut cibum sumere non valeret *Taeg* **4** cibum] cibi *P1 P3 Tr* cum] *add.* autem *Taeg*

5   tribus tandem uicibus de aqua gustans. que reliquiarum martyris fuerat sacrata contactu: primo quidem multum. secundo magis. tertio sensit et exclamauit se fore penitus liberatum. et ex eadem aqua loco doloris abluto: protinus ab omni dolore quieuit: ambulauit fortiter: et cum letitia cibum sumpsit. Quapropter uille illius incole. ingenti
10   admiratione commoti; cum clericis intrauerunt ecclesiam. et campanis pulsantibus: te deum laudamus deuote ad gloriam dei et honorem martyris cantauerunt.

de curatione tumoris per totum corpus cuiusdam pueri

Non fuit autem minoris admirationis: liberatio cuiusdam pueri: de uilla quadam ymalecensis episcopatus. nam cum tanta inflatione per totum corpus esset deformis ut ad uidendum foret terribile: et mors eius potius quam uita a propriis parentibus optaretur. qui iam de
5   salute sperare desiderant. Aqua salutifera. lotus a matre et aliquibus stillis de ipsa gustatis. illico totus detumuit: et insperate restitutus est sanitati.

De curatione alterius spumantis.

In eadem dyocesis. de eadem aqua mirabilioris curationis signum apparuit. Puer enim quidam dictus helyas. cum ante mensam cuiusdam nobilis luderet. in domo et uilla eiusdem a quadam egritudine subito arreptus. et in terram prostratus. linguam cum
5   spuma extra os in longum eiciens. ita ipsam atrociter mordebat

---

5 uicibus] diebus *Taeg*   6 sacrata contactu] contactu consecrata *Taeg* | contactu] *add.* et *P1 exp.* | secundo] secundum *Taeg*   7 ex] *om. Taeg*   9 cum letitia] *om. Taeg* | sumpsit] *add.* cum letitia *Taeg*   11 pulsantibus] pulsatis *Taeg* | ad…12 cantauerunt] cantaverunt, ad Sancti Martyris Petri, & Dei gloriam qui facit mirabilia magna solus. *Taeg*   13 per…pueri] *add.* et doloris pedis ac tibie per aquam predicatam. lxx. *F* | cuiusdam pueri] *om. P1 P2 Tr* add lxix. *P1 W add.* lxix capitulum *N*   **IX.iii,1** fuit autem] *om. Taeg*   2 ymalecensis] Imlacensis *Taeg* episcopatus] diocesis in prefata prouincia fuit *Taeg* | inflatione] esset *Taeg om. P2 S F Ps N W*   3 esset] *add.* inflatione *P2 S F Ps N W Taeg* | foret] esset *P1 P3 Tr* terribile] horribile *Taeg* orribilis *S* horribilis *F Ps N W Nv*   4 uita] *add.* etiam *S exp.* | propriis] *om. Taeg*   5 salutifera] *add.* que reliquiarum Sancti Martyris fuerat contactu consecrata *Taeg*   6 de…gustatis] gustatis de ipsa *P1 P3 Tr* | totus] subito

Martyr's relics. On the first day he felt better, on the second day there was more improvement, and on the third he felt and declared himself fully healed. He washed his tumor with the same water and immediately the pain was relieved, and he was able to walk with strength, and he ate with joy. On account of this the inhabitants of the village, moved by marvelous wonder, went with the clerics into the church and rang the bells, and they began to devoutly sing the *Te Deum*, to the glory of God and the holy Martyr.

On the cure of a boy afflicted with tumors throughout his body IX.iii

Not less amazing was the cure of a certain boy of a town in the Emly diocese. He was afflicted by a terrible swelling in his whole body so that he was horrible to look at and his parents thought death preferable to life in such a state, yet they dared to hope for some remedy, so the mother washed him in the saving water and he tasted any that dripped off. Suddenly the swelling decreased and, as she had hoped, he was restored to health.

On the cure of one foaming at the mouth IX.iv

In the same province and diocese appeared the sign of a still more amazing cure regarding the same water. Before eating the son of the previously mentioned Elias was playing with a certain nobleman of the same house and town, and he was suddenly seized by a pain, and lay prostrate on the ground, his mouth biting down hard on his

---

IX.iii,1 Not…IX.iii,7 health] Taegio, 14.109.   **IX.iv,1** In…IX.iv,16 unprofitable] Taegio, 14.109.

Taeg | et] *om. Taeg*   **7** sanitati] *add.* meritis gloriosi Martyris. *Taeg*   **8** De… IX.xiii,9 secuta] *om. Tr* | spumantis] *add.* lxx. *Pı W add.* per aquam predictam *F add.* lxx capitulum *N*   **IX.iv,1** In…IX.iv,2 apparuit] *om. Taeg*   **2** enim] *om. Taeg* quidam] *add.* in prefata provincia et diocesi nominata *Taeg* | dictus helyas] Henricus nomine *Taeg*   **4** prostratus] *add.* et *Pı* | cum…5 spuma] *om. Taeg* **5** ipsam] *om. Taeg* | atrociter] acriter illam *Taeg*

intrinsecus. ut ex dolore tumescens: post modicum non iam lingua hominis. sed potius bouis aut equi pre magnitudine uideretur. Cumque circumstantes timerent: eam sibimet in breui. dentium constrictione sectandam; nec ipsam aliquatenus intus ualerent 10 reponere: uix tandem in os eius impediente tumore aliquantulum de aqua martyris immiserunt. Quod cum instante iam nocte fecissent. eodem sero linguam retraxit; omni prorsus inflatione carentem. Expedite locutus est: et plena salute recepta. cum gaudio cibum sumpsit. Quod uidentes qui aderant. stupore circumdati: aquam 15 talem reseruare non inutiliter curauerunt.

De facilitate partus per dictam aqua.

Ab uxore namque predicti nobilis sollicite reseruata sed a domino mirabiliter conseruata ita quod post triennium recens et limpida est reperta: Dum ab uxore cuiusdam roberti palmiferi fuisset in partus difficultate potata. uisa est ei omnem dulcedinem superare: et eidem 5 contulit quod excessit utriusque uirtutem. scilicet. faciliter continuo pariendi.

De mirabili conseruatione eiusdem aque inter incendia ignis.

Quedam etiam alia domina eneborgna nomine non oblita quod similis aqua primogenitum suum nomine patricium a mortis discrimine liberaratur; cum eam similiter sollicite reseruasset: mirabilius fuit a domino conseruata. Nam cum casu ignis egressus 5 domos quas petrus maritus eius habebat. in limericensi diocesi.

---

6 ut] *om. Taeg* | tumescens] *add.* ut *Taeg* | iam] *om. Taeg* **7** potius...aut] *om. Taeg* | bouis] boui *P1* **9** aliquatenus intus] *transp. Taeg* | ualerent...10 reponere] *transp. Taeg* **10** impediente tumore] *om. P1 P3* **12** linguam] *add.* suam *Taeg* **13** Expedite] Expediteque *Taeg* | salute] sanitate *Taeg* **14** aquam...15 reseruare] reseruare aquam talem *Taeg* **15** reseruare] *add.* et tam mirabilem *Taeg* curauerunt] crediderunt *Taeg* **16** dictam aqua] aquam predictam. lxii. *F* predictam aqua *N* | aqua] *add.* lxxi. *P1 W* **IX.v,1** Ab...IX.v,3 fuisset] Mulier quedam, uxor cujusdam Roberti Palmiferi, in Hibernia, cum de aqua B. Petri Mart. supradicta bibisset, *Taeg* | reseruata] *add.* est *exp. P1* **3** Dum] Dum cum *P1* **4** omnem] *add.* mellis *Taeg* **5** faciliter] add et *exp. P1* **7** De...ignis] De uase ab igne preseruate

tongue which was protruding from his mouth. Immediately it began to swell so that after a while it appeared not as the tongue of a man, but of a cow or a horse. And when the bystanders became terrified that he might bite it off, they were unable to put the tongue back in his mouth. Someone thought to put little of the Martyr's water in his mouth to hinder the tumor. The night that this was done his tongue relaxed and all the swelling dissipated, and thus unencumbered he began to speak, and he received the full return of his health and took food with joy. Those who were present – the stunned bystanders – believed that to reserve water which was productive of such great miracles was not unprofitable.

On the power of the water to effect easy delivery   IX.v

The wife of the above nobleman carefully preserved the water, and it was miraculously preserved, even after three years it was clear and fresh. A woman, the wife of one Robert Palmer in Ireland, drank the water when she had a difficulty in childbirth, and it seemed to her that it exceeded the sweetness of honey. It comforted her so that she had the strength to continue the birth with ease.

On the wondrous preservation of the water from a fire   IX.vi

Another Lady named Everborga, not forgetting that the water had delivered her firstborn son named Patrick from the danger of death, reserved some similarly with care; it was preserved most marvellously by the Lord. And when by chance a fire consumed houses owned by her husband Peter in the diocese of Limerick, among the burnt ashes

---

IX.v,3 A... 6 ease] Taegio, 14.110.   **IX.vi,1** Another... IX.vi,10 complete] Taegio, 14.110.

---

uirtute ipsius aque. lxxiii. *F add.* lxxii capitulum *N* | ignis] *add.* lxxii. *P1 W*
IX.vi,1 domina] *om. P1 P3* | eneborgna nomine] nomine Everborga in prefata provincia Hiberni *Taeg* **2** similis] supradicta *Taeg* | aqua] *add.* B. Petri Mart. reliquiis consecrata *Taeg* | patricium] Petrum *Taeg* **3** liberaratur] liberaverat *Taeg* sollicite] *om. Taeg* **4** casu] *add.* fuisset *P1*

consumpsisset; inter ipsos incendii cineres. uas ligneum in quo reposita fuerat: quodam incredibili modo integrum et incombustum repertum est. Cumque fuisset in aliud uas translata: primum protinus in cinerem est redactum. Quod factum euidenter edocuit. ob cuius

10 gratiam uas pristinum fuerat in sua integritate seruatum.

De pluribus a pluribus imfirmitatibus per eandem aquam.

In eadem quoque diocesi. et ciuitate plures a pluribus infirmitatibus. et diuersi diuersimode liberati sunt. Nam in eadem dyocesis limirecensi. uxor cuiusdam ioannis deudeuonella. cum amissa iam loquela uideretur mortem singultibus peruenire: potu eiusdem aque

5 salutaris loquendi officio et saluti fuit pariter restituta.

Altera mulier in ciuitate post potum aque prefate. uomens spurcitie non modicam quantitatem: a quodam mortis repentino miraculo liberatur.

altera uero simili nomine letitia uocata; ut uir quoque letitia de sua letificaretur salute: per similem potum et uomitum a quadam antiqua egritudine de qua desperauerat. consecuta est sanitatem.

Ibidem etiam per potum eiusdem aque secunda leticia cum duabus aliis mulieribus que multis doloribus et angustiis grauibus cruciabantur in partu: faciliter et leuiter postmodum pepererunt.

---

6 quo] *add.* supradicta aqua *Taeg* 7 incredibili] mirabili *Taeg* | incombustum] incorruptum *Taeg* 9 cinerem] cineres *Taeg* 10 fuerat] *om. Taeg* | seruatum] conseruatum fuit *Taeg* 11 De...aquam] De quadam malore uirtute ispius aque a mortis periculo liberata. lxxiiii *F* | aquam] *add.* lxxiii. *P1 W add.* lxxiii capitulum *N* **IX.vii,1** In... IX.vii,2 sunt] *om. Taeg* 2 Nam] *om. Taeg* | dyocesis] prouincia , in diocesi *Taeg* 3 deudeuonella] dedondouenolla *F S Ps N W* Donevola *Taeg* dondo uenolla *Nv* 4 aque...5 salutaris] *transp. Taeg* 5 saluti] salutis s *exp. P1* restituta] *add.* lxxiiii. *P1 W add.* de quibusdam mulieribus per ipsam aquam miraculose curate. lxxv. *F* **IX.viii,2** quodam mortis] *transp. Taeg add.* periculo *Taeg* | miraculo] *om. Taeg* **IX.ix,1** nomine] *add.* scilicet *Taeg* | uocata] uocata uocatur *Taeg* 3 qua] *add.* iam *Taeg* | desperauerat] *add.* plenam *Taeg* **IX.x,1** Ibidem... IX.x,2 mulieribus] in eadem provincia Hiberni tres mulieres *Taeg* 2 aliis] *om. P1 P3* 3 et leuiter] leuiterque *Taeg* | pepererunt] *add.* per similem aque potum meritisque Martyris sancti. *Taeg add.* lxxv. *P1 W add.* De simile curationem

was the wooden pot in which the water had been placed, and the wonder was that it was found whole and unburned. When the water was put into another vase, the first one immediately was reduced to ashes. This manifestly teaches that it was by his grace that the vase was preserved complete.

Of the cure of many sicknesses through the water   IX.vii

In the same diocese and city many were cured of different ailments and various sicknesses. In the diocese of Limerick, the wife of a certain John Donevola was overcome with tears since he had lost his voice and seemed dead. After having drunk this salutary water, he recovered the power of speech and was completely restored to health.

Another woman in the same city, after drinking the water, vomited a   IX.viii
vast quantity of filth, and was delivered from the sudden danger of death.

Another was similarly called Laetitia – so that a man might also   IX.ix
rejoice with happiness in her healing – through a similar drink vomited up a certain old affliction, of which she was already despairing, and complete health followed.

In the same province of Ireland there was a second Laetitia who with   IX.x
two other women had suffered great pangs in childbirth. After they had taken drinks of the water they afterwards had easy and joyful childbirths.

IX.vii,1 In … IX.vii,5 health] Taegio, 14.108. **IX.viii,1** Another … 3 death] Taegio, 14.109. **IX.ix,1** Another … 4 followed] Taegio, 14.109. **IX.x,1** In … 4 childbirths] Taegio, 14.110.

---

alterius mulieris. lxxvi *F* *add.* de liberatione cuiusdam alterius mulieris per predictam aquam. lxxv capitulum *N*

In laoniensi. quoque dyocesi quedam nomine christina uxor gilberti anglici a simile periculo per simile miraculum fuit subito liberata. lxxvi.

Ceterum quedam alia nomine basilia uxor ioannis cognomento lepoer. cum remansisset ita uehementer tumefacta post partum quod se credebat iterum paritura; aqua supradicta cum deuotione suscepta: continuo tumor et timor mortis ab ea pariter discesserunt.

Adhuc euidentius miraculum claruit per aquam martyris in eadem diocesi laoniensi. Ibi namque mulier quedam nobilis nomine illitia. ita usum lingue omniumque sensuum perdiderat et persone uiuentis colorem: ut iam mortua uideretur. Quod cum per duos dies in tali mortificatione stetisset. omnia in se mortis fere signa pretendens. et ei cilicium et alia que sunt necessaria funeri pararentur; postquam de aqua uirtuosa portauit uel gustauit mox loquelam et sensus omnes recuperauit amissos. uiuidus color restitutus est. perfecta demum liberatione secuta.

Talibus aqua miraculis in hybernia aliorum elementorum testimoniis consona. preconia martyris extollebat: sed nichilominus aliis signis pluribus in eadem prouincia merita martyris refulserunt.

IX.xi,1 laoniensi] lanoniensi prim. n *exp. Pi* | dyocesi] *add.* prefate provinci, *Taeg*
2 a] per *Pi* | liberata] *add.* de curatione cuiusdam mulieris tumefacta per aquam predictam. lxxvii *F add.* Item de liberatione cuiusdam alterius mulieris. lxxvi capitulum *N add.* lxxvi *W* **IX.xii,1** Ceterum] *om. Taeg* | alia nomine] *om. Taeg*
2 lepoer] Epoes *Taeg* | tumefacta…partum] post partum tumefacta *Taeg* **3** se credebat] *transp. Taeg* | deuotione] *add.* et fide *Taeg* **4** tumor] *add.* predictus ac *Taeg* | timor mortis] *transp. Taeg* | discesserunt] *add.* lxxvii. *Pi add.* de curatione feminine iam priuate uerbo et motu per aquam predictam. lxxviii. *F add.* de curatione feminine iam priuate uerbo et motu. lxxvii capitulum. *N W* **IX.xiii,1** Adhuc…IX.xiii,1 eadem] in prouincia Hiberni in *Taeg* **2** Ibi namque] *om. Taeg* | nomine illitia] *transp. Taeg* **3** sensuum] membrorum *Taeg* **4** colorem] calorem *Taeg* | ut] *add.* s *exp. Pi* | Quod] que *F S Ps N W* **5** mortis fere] *transp. Taeg* **6** alia…pararentur] ea que funeri necessaria sunt, pararentur *Taeg* **7** portauit uel] que reliquiarum Martyris contactu fuerat consecrata, *Taeg om. F S Ps N W Nv* | et sensus] sensusque *Taeg* **8** uiuidus color] uiuidusque calor *Taeg* est] et *Taeg* **9** liberatione] liberati est *Taeg* | secuta] *add.* lxxviii. *Pi W* de diuersis

In the diocese of Killaloe, Christina, the wife of Gilbert of England, was suddenly freed from a similar danger by a like miracle.

IX.xi

Another one named Basilia, the wife of John Epoes, had remained terribly swollen after birth, so that she believed she might give birth to twins, and she took the water with devotion, and at once the swelling dissipated and her fear of death decreased.

IX.xii

Besides this a more evident miracle happened through the martyr's water in the same diocese of Killaloe, where there was a woman named Illicia who first had lost the use of speech for a long time and finally lost the complexion proper to a living person so that she seemed to be dead. Since she had remained so subdued for two days – all signs pointing that she was near death – all the sheets and things which were necessary for a funeral were prepared. After she had tasted the powerful water, suddenly she recovered all her lost speech and feeling, and her color was restored and at length full restoration of health followed.

IX.xiii

By such miracles in Ireland did water extol the praises of the martyr which are consonant with the testimonies of the other elements. But nonetheless many other signs shined forth in that province by the merits of the martyr.

IX.xiv

IX.xi,1 In…2 miracle] Taegio, 14.110. **IX.xii,1** Another…4 decreased] Taegio, 14.110. **IX.xiii,1** Besides…10 followed] Taegio, 14.108.

---

miraculis per ipsum in hybernia factus. lxxix *F add.* lxxviii capitulum *N* **IX.xiv,3** refulserunt] *add.* lxxix. *P1 add.* de aliis quibusdam miraculis in eadem prouincia. lxxx *F add.* de aliis quibusdam miraculis in eadem prouincia. lxxix capitulum *N*

Quidam namque puer febre laborans grauissima. sic ad extrema
deductus. quod uix perpendi posset utrum caloris in eius precordiis.
aut in ore aliquid remansisset. et iam a parentibus tamquam mortuus
ploraretur: emisso uoto per martyri deuote recommendatus secundum
5 consuetudinem patrie mensuratus: mox calorem recuperauit et
alitum. et paulo post integram sanitatem.

Alio etiam cuiusdam mulieris limericensis filio ad ecclesiam fratrum
predicatorum in eadem ciuitate portato. ut martyris reliquias uisitaret:
ipsis uisis illico reddita est ei potentia quam perdiderat ambulandi: Et
sic matri cui prius fuerat onus et tedium: factus est socius postea
5 itineris et solamen.

Sed et quidam frater predicatorum nomine enuinus. cum haberet
alterum de genibus ita lesum. quod sine baculi adminiculo ambulare
non posset; uoto emisso se conuertens ad martyrem quod de ipso in
uesperis et matutinis de cetero memoriam faceret. si eum meritis
5 ipsius dominus liberasset: confestim uoti sensibiliter perpendens
effectum. Postmodum perfecte curatus: illius memor esse non desiit
preco et testis uirtutum eius effectus.

IX.xv,1 Quidam... IX. xvii,7 effectus] *om. Tr* | namque] *om. Taeg* | laborans] *om.*
Taeg 2 deductus] *add.* est *Taeg* | quod] ut *Taeg* | utrum] *add.* quid *Taeg* 3 aut] et
Taeg | aliquid] *add. al. man. sup.* liquidum *P2* | tamquam] quasi *Taeg*
4 ploraretur] plangeretur *Taeg* | emisso] *om. Taeg* | emisso... martyri] *om. F*
martyri] *add.* sancto *Taeg* | deuote recommendatus] *transp. Taeg* | recommendatus]
add. martyri *P2 F S Ps N W Nv* 6 alitum] anelitum *P1* halitum *Taeg* | sanitatem]
add. lxxx. *P1* de curatione cuiusdam qui perdiderat usum ambulandi. lxxxi. *F add.*
lxxx capitulum *N* IX.xvi,1 Alio] Filio *F S Ps N W Nv* | Alio... IX.xvi,1 filio] Filio
cuiusdam militis *Taeg* | filio] *om. F S Ps N W Nv* 2 eadem] *om. Taeg* | ciuitate]
add. Limericensi *Taeg* 3 reddita est] *transp. Taeg* | ei] *om. F S Ps N W Nv* | ei...
ambulandi] ambulandi potentia quam perdiderat *Taeg* 4 prius fuerat] *transp. Taeg*
onus] bonus *P1* b *exp.* | socius] *om. Taeg* | socius postea] *transp. P2 F S Ps N W*
5 itineris] utilis *P1 P2 P3* | solamen] *add.* lxxxi *P1 W add.* De liberatione cuiusdam
fratris ordinis predicatorum. lxxxii. *F add.* lxxxi capitulum. IX. xvii,1 Sed...
quidam] *om. Taeg* | frater] *add.* quidam de Ordine *Taeg* | nomine enuinus] *om.*
Taeg | enuinus] neuus *P2* neuimus *F S Ps N W Nv* 2 alterum] *om. Taeg* | de] ex

A little boy had a very severe fever so that he was at the point of IX.xv
death. It was so serious that it was difficult to assess whether there was
any warmth left in his vitals or if any moisture remained in his
mouth. Already his parents were mourning his death, while the
mother made a vow to the holy Martyr, according to the devout
custom of the place. Suddenly the boy recovered warmth and breath
and a little later fullness of health.

Another woman of Limerick carried her son to the church of the IX.xvi
Friars Preachers in the city of Limerick, in order to visit the Martyr's
relics. Upon seeing them he was immediately able to walk, an ability
which he had previously lost. And so, for the mother to whom he had
been a burden and weariness, he was now made a companion in the
journey home and source of comfort.

Also a brother of the order of Preachers named Éimhín had hurt one IX.xvii
of his knees so badly that he was unable to walk without the aid of a
staff. He made an oath and turned himself towards the Martyr,
promised that he would commit to memory his Vespers and Lauds in
all respects, if the Lord would free him through his merits, and was
immediately healed. Ever after he was always mindful of the favor,
keeping in mind the deed that had been accomplished.

IX.xv,1 A…7 health] Taegio, 11.87. **IX.xvi,1** Another…IX.xvii,1] Taegio,
13.100. **IX.xvii,1** Also…7 accomplished] Taegio, 9.68.

Taeg | Iesum] *add.* haberet *Taeg* **3** uoto emisso] *transp. Taeg* **4** matutinis]
Laudibus *Taeg* **5** uoti] non *Taeg* | perpendens] perpendit *Taeg* **6** effectum] *add.*
Qui *Taeg add.* et *F S Ps N W Nv* | curatus] sanatus *Taeg* **7** preco…effectus]
postmodum virtutum ipsius testis effectus *Taeg* | effectus] *add.* lxxxii. *P1 W add.*
Quia multa alia miracula per ipsum facta sunt. lxxxiii. *F add.* lxxxii capitulum *N*

X   Multa etiam alia signa fecit dominus per martyrem suum: que in hoc opusculo non sunt scripta. hec autem scripta sunt ut credatis; et credentes uitam habeatis in nomine ipsius. qui in medio ecclesie os eius apperuit in doctrinis. et impleuit eum spiritu intellectus et

5   sapientie in scripturis: et stola glorie induit eum pro stola innocentie uirginalis. et pro palma triumphalis uictorie iocunditatem et exultationem thesaurizauit super eum in celo: et nomine eterno hereditauit illum in mundo dominus deus noster. cui est honor et gloria in secula seculorum amen.

X.i,1 Multa...dominus] Jn 20:30   **3** in² ... 5 induit] Sir 15:5; Introit of the liturgy for the Common of Doctors   **6** iocunditatem...8 illum] Sir 15:6

X.i,1 alia] *om. Tr*   **2** et] *add.* ut *Tr*   **3** os...4 apperuit] aperuit os eius *Tr*   **4** spiritu] *add.* et. *F add.* sapientie et *exp. P1*   **5** stola²] palma *S*   **8** in mundo] *om. P2* **9** amen] *add.* hanc legendam beati petri martiris compilauit frater Thomas de Agni de ordinis predicatorum. et sunt ibi. lxxxiii. miracula pulcra ualde. et diuuiduntur per capitula ut melius cognoscantur. et si semel in mense legerentur in mensa. esset utile ualde fratribus: et bona et utilis materia ad predicandum. et ad alia. *P2 add.* Explicit legenda sancti petri martiris de ordine fratrum predicatorum composita fratrem thomam de lentino patriarcham iherusolimitam. *F add.* Explicit legenda sancti petri martiris de ordine fratrum predicatorum *N add.* Deo gratias *W*

The Lord worked many other signs through His martyr which are not written in this work. Those that are written, are written so that you might believe, and by believing, might have life in His name, (Jn 20:30) Our Lord and God, who opened his mouth in the midst of the Church (Sir 15:5) in doctrine, and filled him with the spirit of wisdom and understanding in the scriptures, and who endowed him with the garment of glory through the robe of virginal innocence and the triumphal palm of victory, and enriched him with joy and exultation and caused him to inherit an everlasting name (Sir 15:6) in the world, to whom be honor and glory for endless ages. Amen.

The official *Vita* of Peter of Verona by Friar Thomas Agni of Lentini from the mid-1260s is here presented with a critical edition and translation for the first time; all extant witnesses to the text have been consulted. After his assassination in 1252, Peter of Verona was rapidly proclaimed a martyr, and his *Vita* testifies to the far-reaching extension of his cult, spreading out from Italy and Southern France to reach western Iberia and Ireland, as is attested by the miracles attributed to his intercession. Donald Prudlo has previously provided the first edition of the *Summa contra hereticos* attributed to Peter Martyr, published as Medium Ævum Monographs new series XXXVIII (2020).

Cover image: detail from Pedro Berruguete, *San Pedro Mártir* (1490s), Museo del Prado (Wikipedia; public-domain image).

ISBN 978-1-911694-09-0

90000

9 781911 694090

www.ingramcontent.com/pod-product-compliance
Lightning Source LLC
Chambersburg PA
CBHW060310100426
42812CB00003B/721